IS
HUMAN
FORGIVENESS
POSSIBLE?

IS
HUMAN
FORGIVENESS
POSSIBLE?

A Pastoral Care Perspective

JOHN PATTON

Abingdon Press
Nashville

IS HUMAN FORGIVENESS POSSIBLE?

Library of Congress Cataloging-in-Publication Data

PATTON, JOHN, 1930–
   Is human forgiveness possible?
   Includes index.
   1. Forgiveness. I. Title.
   BJ1476.P37   1985   241'.4   85-9191
                  ISBN 0-687-19704-X
                  (soft: alk. paper)

Scripture quotations in this publication are from the Revised
Standard Version of the Bible, copyrighted 1946, 1952, © 1971,
1973 by the Division of Christian Education of the National Council
of the Churches of Christ in the U.S.A. and are used by permission.

MANUFACTURED BY THE PARTHENON PRESS AT
NASHVILLE, TENNESSEE, UNITED STATES OF AMERICA

To the generation before,
John and Vera,
and the generation after,
Becky, Marc, Joanna, and Tim,
who have been in special relation to me

Acknowledgments

My awareness of the problem this book addresses grew out of my experience as a pastor; therefore, my indebtedness is to that experience and to those who helped place me in positions where I could acquire it. This is where pastoral theology begins and where it returns to strengthen the practice of ministry. My first thoughts about some of the issues in this book came in response to two articles by my friend James Lapsley that were published back in the sixties and to which I refer later in the book. My first opportunity to think out loud about the problem of human forgiveness came in a symposium honoring another friend, my former clinical pastoral education supervisor, Obert Kempson. The first version of the thesis of the book and some of the case material appeared in my article in the Kempson Symposium published by the Association of Mental Health Clergy in *Cura Animarum: A Journal for the Advancement of Religious Care of Troubled Persons*, volume 36, number 1 (May 1984) and used here with permission.

I express my indebtedness to a number of persons for reading all or part of the manuscript and offering support and suggestions: Ben Kline, Charles Cousar, Calvin Kropp, David Abernathy, and Carl Holladay. Their suggestions, though not always followed, were much appreciated. Finally, with this book, as well as with most everything in my life, I acknowledge my indebtedness to Helen, my wife, who read the manuscript for intelligibility. Her marginal comments about why in the world I would want to say something like that helped me to make the book far better than it would have been otherwise.

Contents

Introduction

Although it may seem presumptuous for a pastoral theologian—rather than a biblical or systematic one—to be writing about forgiveness, in many ways I have no choice about dealing with it. My particular ministry continually presents the problem to me, and consequently, I am forced to make some kind of judgments about it. Moreover, I believe that concerns about human forgiveness are confronted by any caring pastor who takes seriously the vocation both to care for human hurts and to represent forgiveness as a possibility in life. This book is, therefore, an effort to address an issue I confront in my ministry almost every day.

How does one convey the possibility of human forgiveness to those who find themselves unable to forgive? "Not very easily" has been the answer I have had to give. My counselees—and I don't think they are very different from most people—have usually thought of the possibility of forgiving someone who has injured them as at best an "impossible possibility." The bind I have felt in my response Niebuhr to them has been between my attempt to respond sensitively to the rage and pain that they feel, yet at the same time to take seriously the reality and importance of human forgiveness as it appears in the Gospels. I suspect that I am not alone in my experience of that problem.

It is valuable for pastors to examine human forgiveness both because of the centrality of the problem in human relationships and also because of insights such an examination offers about the nature of pastoral counseling. To examine the issues surrounding human forgiveness requires us to consider rage and shame as well as interpersonal power and righteousness. These certainly affect forgiveness. They are also involved in many other dimensions of pastoral counseling. Moreover, examining a problem as central to Christian faith as human forgiveness can underscore one of the most important principles about pastoral counseling. The ministry of pastoral counseling is not primarily an attempt to solve problems, even this problem.

That human forgiveness is a problem, however, does need to be recognized. Perhaps because forgiveness has been so important to the church, acknowledging that there is a problem with it has sometimes been seen to be an act of unfaithfulness. Human forgiveness has generally been understood as something Christians do and which the church helps them in doing. The Lord's Prayer, for example, speaks of forgiving our debts and debtors. Nevertheless, in over twenty years of pastoral counseling, what I have heard again and again (even from those for whom the prayer was most important) is, "I just can't forgive her (or him) for what she (or he) has done." There are some issues which simply cannot be addressed by trying harder.

In order to examine human forgiveness as it appears in pastoral counseling, I begin the first chapter by presenting two case fragments, both of which suggest the importance and difficulty of human forgiveness. In addition to illustrating the problem, the cases also point in the direction of what seems to me to be its resolution—forgiveness discovered rather than done. At this point in the book, however, there is no detailed interpretation of the cases. They are simply used to identify some of the issues which make human forgiveness a problem.

The case material, however, immediately reveals some of

the special characteristics of relationships within the family. Whatever the presenting problem, every person whom I have seen in counseling is also finishing an old agenda with a parent or working out where he or she is in relation to a mate—usually both. Having a sound and practically useful way of thinking about these relationships is profoundly important for both the pastor and the counselee, for there is something special about such relationships that affects every norm for behavior, including human forgiveness. The case material reveals some of the special characteristics of these two intimate human relationships. In them one cannot either act or be a certain way on the basis of general theological or ethical principles alone. The nature of the relationship significantly affects what one is or does more than any principles guiding one's behavior. A significant part of the problem with human forgiveness, therefore, is how these two relationships affect such principles.

The act which calls for forgiveness usually causes guilt in the injuring person and shame in the person injured by that act; therefore, the next dimension of the problem to be examined is shame as it relates to guilt. My experience in pastoral counseling has been that although most persons talk about guilt, theirs or someone else's, their most profound experience is with shame. Guilt can more nearly be dealt with according to rational principle, whereas shame is inevitably relational and personal and, as such, even more related to the special relationships of the family. Perhaps because of the long association of guilt with forgiveness in the Christian tradition, the effect of shame upon human forgiveness has been insufficiently examined. This is the rationale for the extensive discussion of shame in the second chapter of the book. I believe that pastors need to know more about shame and its relation to human selfhood if they are to offer effective care to troubled persons.

Like most pastoral counselors, I spend much of my time in dealing with the defenses persons erect to defend themselves against powerful human experiences, such as shame. Chapters 3 and 4, therefore, discuss some of the ways in which persons defend themselves against shame:

[13]

rage

withholding power to forgive

with rage, power, and righteousness. Understanding the rage produced by shame is the first step toward understanding how persons attempt to defend themselves against that experience. Two of the psychological defenses against shame—power (the power to forgive) and righteousness (the insistence that one is right in a situation of injury to the self)—have particular interest for the pastoral theologian because they appear to be supported by religion. Someone who has been hurt may derive a significant degree of power from withholding forgiveness from the injuring person if that person has sufficient guilt. Even if the extent of the other person's guilt is not known, there is a fantasied power over the other person in the belief that forgiveness is indeed something that one can give or withhold. This fantasy is amplified in popular religion's viewing forgiveness simply as something that one does, and it is further distorted by emphasizing the power of that function rather than its revelation of our common human condition. The dynamics of power are related both to the self's infantile omnipotence and its struggle for autonomy, which religion often supports through exhortations for forgiveness. How one gives up the power to forgive is a central problem with human forgiveness.

righteousness as defense

The other defense against shame which I examine in some detail is righteousness or, more popularly stated, being right. This defense also appears to be supported by religion. The church has a long history of attempting to determine who is right in a particular human situation such as divorce or conflict between parents and children. Psychologically, however, righteousness functions in another way. If one cannot be loved, then he or she can find satisfaction in being right or righteous. "You may have rejected me, but I know that I am right." In the special relationships of the family and even in less personal relationships, the need to be right is a major contributor to the problem with human forgiveness.

Chapter 5 examines the problem with human forgiveness as it appears in discussions of forgiveness itself. Forgiveness has, for example, most often been understood as an attitude and/or an act, and there are difficulties with both of those views. An overconcern by the church for confession and catharsis is also a problem. The search for guilt can reduce the pastor's awareness of shame and some of the broader issues of what it means to be human. To move toward my constructive position, I use interpretations by pastoral theologians of forgiveness as a process of realization, of its relation to law and gospel and to reconciliation. The chapter concludes with a reintroduction of the case material and a suggestion of how it can contribute to the thesis that human forgiveness is more discovery than act.

The final chapter examines the relation of human and divine forgiveness and how a New Testament view of forgiveness can be related to the lives of persons to whom the pastor offers care and counseling. I attempt to relate the case material to the point of view which emerges from the New Testament in interpreting the primary emphasis of Jesus' teaching, the kingdom of God. Following chapter 6 are some concluding reflections which attempt to show how the discovery of common humanity imaged both in the New Testament and in the case material can offer specific help for persons struggling with human forgiveness.

There are a number of limitations to this exploration of the problem with human forgiveness in pastoral counseling which are related to the background, experience, and bias of the author. One conscious limitation is the decision to omit a detailed consideration of the relation between forgiveness and reconciliation, which traditionally have been discussed together. Although I make a number of statements using the concept of reconciliation, I focus upon forgiveness alone because it is the theological concept of which my counselees are most aware. Another limitation is the book's focus upon issues in the pastoral care of individuals, couples, and families. As a pastor who specializes in pastoral counseling, I am writing for other pastors who minister to persons in a variety of settings. Although much of the discussion of human forgiveness and the problems surrounding it seems to me to have implications for theology and the ethics of human relations which extend beyond the special relations of the family, my specific concern in this book is with developing an understanding of human forgiveness for pastoral counseling. Nevertheless, because forgiveness is an issue that faces "all sorts and conditions" of persons, much of the discussion has relevance for anyone who is aware of and concerned with the problem.

What I hope to demonstrate in the book is that the issues raised in persons' struggles with forgiving cut across the whole spectrum of human relationships, and that a more adequate understanding of some of the most important of them is essential for pastors and for those to whom they minister. Examining the problem with human forgiveness as it appears in pastoral counseling can contribute significantly to the quality of care which pastors can offer to troubled persons. As I attempt to relate pastoral experience and theological interpretation, my specific thesis about human forgiveness is that *human forgiveness is not doing something but discovering something—that I am more like those who have hurt me than different from them. I am able to forgive when I discover that I am in no position to forgive. Although the experience of God's forgiveness may involve confession of, and the sense of being forgiven for, specific sins, at its heart it is the recognition of my reception into the community of sinners—those affirmed by God as his children.*

[16]

Human Forgiveness in the Family

F orgive us our sins—*that we may forgive even those in special relation to us.*

Emmie and Tom are two of the persons with whom I have experienced the problem of human forgiveness. With Emmie the problem involved the marital relationship; with Tom, relationship to a parent. I share a portion of their stories in order to show how I have experienced the bind with human forgiveness in pastoral counseling. The details of the stories have been changed to make it impossible to identify either person, but because we are so much alike, they may seem very familiar.

Emmie is the fifty-year-old wife of a Presbyterian elder who, without saying anything to her beforehand, left home and moved in with another woman. After Elmer left, he never came back, so that much of the time prior to the divorce, Emmie did not know where he was. She, who had given nearly thirty years of her life to marriage and children, was left without either. (The children had grown up and moved away.) Emmie talked with her pastor, who was impressed enough by the depth of her hurt and her cold, quiet rage that he referred her to me for further pastoral counseling.

I spent more than two years in pastoral counseling with Emmie, seeing her—after the first few months—every other week. It was not what one would call intensive psycho-therapy, but it was an intensive relationship. What Emmie felt for me was not simply transference of feelings from the past, but a real, loving relationship which served as a partial substitute for what she had lost. In spite of my importance to Emmie, however, I was never able to help her work through her rage toward her former husband. She talked about it a lot and extended the anger to her children when they insisted on caring about their father in spite of what he had done to her. When they came to town on a visit, we worked on their relationship together in a family interview. But although some of the communication within the family became more direct, Emmie held tightly to her conviction that she had been wronged and that her strong, Presby-terian God was not doing his job in allowing her husband to go on enjoying life.

She continued to worship in the church, where she taught children in the Sunday school and tried to set a good example. Each Sunday she joined the congregation in praying that fifth petition of the Lord's Prayer, "forgive us our debts as we forgive our debtors," and seemed to continue her unforgiving life. The position of having been grievously wronged continued to be important to her, even though in counseling I sought by various means to undermine that position.

In other ways, however, Emmie's life situation improved. She got a job, improved her relationships with her siblings and her children, came to terms with her mother's death, and fell in love—not just with me this time, but with a married man whom she had met at her place of employment. As she talked of this affair—she did not call it that because she had not had sexual relations with him—what may seem obvious to the reader began to become obvious to me. Perhaps that Presbyterian God had finally allowed her to see herself as a sinner. One day in our regular twice-a-month interview, I said:

Pastor: As I listened to you talking about your relationship to your friend, I found myself wondering if you ever saw yourself as in the same position as Elmer [her husband].

Emmie: (*quickly*) No!

Pastor: Oh, I see. It occurred to me that there might be some similarities.

Emmie: Well, *I* don't see them.

Some therapists might at that point have commented on the intensity of her affect and suggested its meaning, but I decided to wait awhile longer on that Presbyterian God who seemed finally to be getting with it. Elmer, who had moved with his new wife to another city, lost his job and was apparently unable to pay his alimony. Emmie was angry, financially pressed, but to my surprise was able in a letter to express both her anger and her concern about Elmer's job situation. In a matter-of-fact way she described her financial needs and requested resumption of alimony payments as soon as he was re-employed. As she told me about this in our next interview, I commented:

Pastor: Elmer sounds almost human!

Emmie: What?

Pastor: I never had thought of him as an ordinary human being before, but listening to you then, the thought did occur to me. You sounded as if you were concerned about his predicament.

Emmie: Well, he got himself into it.

Pastor: I know. I was just noticing how you sounded. For the first time I can remember, he didn't seem like the enemy—just an ordinary human being. [I sighed and commented that it felt good. Emmie remained silent.]

Although my theological juices were flowing, I was able to keep my mouth shut and not say, "By that slow-working Presbyterian God, I believe you've finally done it." Shortly after that Emmie terminated her relationship with me, suggesting that it was getting in the way of the relationship to her now divorced friend.

I ask the reader to accept this case fragment at this point as simply one of the situations in which I experienced the problem with human forgiveness. My question throughout the experience was, How is the Lord's Prayer's petition to forgive one's debtors related to Emmie? I return to Emmie's story later on with that and other questions in mind.

Tom is a twenty-five-year-old single male whose early experience in counseling with me dealt primarily with his relationship to his father. Although his presenting problem was his relationships to women, things quickly moved to Tom and his father. When Tom was about fourteen or fifteen, his father had an affair, divorced Tom's mother, and left Tom to be the "man of the house." He shared with me the anger he felt at what he perceived as the father's abandonment of him. Perhaps more important, however, were his feelings of impotence and lack of power in relationship to his father and the anger he felt because of that abandonment.

At one point in our relationship when Tom's feelings toward me were quite intense, his father called him about plans for a forthcoming holiday visit. Tom talked with him about some of what he was getting at in counseling and confronted him on the phone with some of the angry feelings he was having. To Tom's surprise, his father shared with him some of his own feelings of weakness and hopelessness prior to his divorce—how he wanted to spend more time with Tom but had felt trapped in the relationship to Tom's mother.

Tom described the lump he felt in his throat when he talked to his father and which he felt now in talking to me. I commented:

Pastor:	What's the lump? Discovering that he had problems too?
Tom:	Wondering if I really can forgive him.
Pastor:	[My theory at this point is that he is hung up on thinking of forgiveness as something he *can* or *cannot* do.] It's hard to give up that power.
Tom:	Power?
Pastor:	You sound more like a priest than a son. Go back to the lump in your throat.
Tom:	What do you mean?

[20]

Pastor: I felt more forgiveness when you told me about the lump than when you began to speculate on whether you could forgive him or not.

Tom: It did seem more real—but scary.

Pastor: Coming down from the seat of power is scary. If your dad is human like you, you might find you can have something more with him than some occasional time together.

Tom: [Moved on to talk about his difficulties in being close in a number of relationships.]

Prior to the interview above, Tom had insisted to his father that he was going to bring his girlfriend, Betty, to the holiday family gathering in spite of his father's saying that that would prevent him and Tom from spending time together. Tom had felt good that he had stood up to his father about this. Now, as the holiday approached, he was having second thoughts. He talked to me about being uncomfortable with Betty and not sure he really wanted to take her.

Pastor: It sounds like you're ashamed of her.

Tom: Yeah. It feels like that.

Pastor: You chose to confront your dad about the importance of bringing Betty, and now it doesn't seem that you have much to show off to them. She's acting weak and dependent upon you.

Tom: I wish it were the way it was when I first met her. Now I'm feeling trapped.

Pastor: Oh! (*expressing some surprise*) Then your father's not the only one in the family who's had to suffer with an inadequate woman. (*pause*) But, of course, you would never be disloyal like he was.

Tom: What do you mean?

Pastor: I was just thinking about how it seemed like you dad left your mother because he felt there was something wrong with her, and how you thought you needed to be better than that.

Tom: (*after some silence*) That feels like it may be it.

Pastor: You may be like the old son-of-a-gun in spite of yourself.

Tom: (*silence*)

Pastor: (*responding to Tom's sad look*) What's your sadness about?

Tom: I don't know. I guess I'm ashamed of being that little and self-centered. I ought to care more for Betty now, but I don't want to.

Pastor: I guess it runs in the family.

Tom: Damn you!

Pastor: (*after a pause*) When your self-righteousness gets punctured, it can be pretty painful.

Tom: You and your theological words. I think of it as selfishness or narcissism.

Pastor: The theological words are more embarrassing to you, so I'm going to stay with them. In fact, your sadness about your lost self-righteousness reminds me of a Bible story.

Tom: Oh, God . . .

Pastor: Actually, I was thinking of the words more than the story. Do you remember the bit about Elijah sitting off by himself, angry and depressed, saying, "Oh, Lord, now take away my life, for I am no better than my fathers"?

Tom: I don't remember, but I know what you mean. I'm not any better. (*long silence*)

Pastor: Do you know what you're feeling?

Tom: Like I'm down in a hole.

Pastor: I was feeling pretty good. Maybe that's just my insensitivity to your pain. (*pause*) No, I don't think so. I believe it's the hope I feel for people when they get in touch with their self-righteousness instead of kidding themselves.

Tom: Well, I'm still worried about going.

Pastor: That's OK, if you enjoy that sort of thing, but it occurred to me that it might be more fun if you could visit your father's family as a vacation instead of as some kind of examination.

Tom: Yeah, that would be great.

In these unique, but very familiar-feeling stories, some of the problem with human forgiveness is revealed. For Emmie, the hurt she felt in the rejection by her husband was paralleled by an earlier feeling of rejection because she had never quite measured up to her mother's expectations. Her way of dealing with this, both with her mother and her husband, was to be good or to do what was right. If she couldn't be sure she was loved, she could at least know that she was doing the right thing. She held on tightly to this view of herself until she could feel love and affirmation as a person through pastoral counseling and other developing relationships. Only then, when she felt affirmed in spite of the shame at being rejected, did something like forgiveness become possible for her.

With Tom the issue was focused more on power than on righteousness—although, as we shall see, the two are very closely related. He was uncertain about his own power as a man and in relation to his father. To substitute for that, he held on to the power to forgive. He was uncertain as to where he was with formal religion. He had grown up in the church but was now estranged from it. Nevertheless, he had some definite assumptions about the importance of forgiveness, and in his uncertainty about himself he held on to both his father's offense against him and his fantasies of at least having the power to forgive or not forgive him.

The Use of Case Material

I have chosen not to present lengthy interpretations of either case at this time, but to return to them throughout the book as well as to make use of other case material to illustrate and inform the theological and psychological issues under consideration. Any use of case material, however, raises the question of just how it is being used or what it means when it is used. What is the authority of Emmie's or Tom's life experience for dealing with the problem of human forgiveness? Moreover, what I am presenting is my interpretation of the case material, not that of Emmie or Tom. Am I claiming that my interpretation of this material is what these stories mean?

Actually, my claim is much more simple. I believe that the experiences of Emmie and Tom raise important questions about the way human forgiveness is commonly understood. The fact that Emmie's and Tom's initial concerns in counseling appear to be different from this does not invalidate the use of their stories. Emmie and Tom do not own or control the meaning of their experience for others any more than a writer can control the interpretation of what he or she writes. The major issue is simply to be sure that the life experience is valued and respected as it is—that it is not forced into other categories that unnecessarily distort it. The authority of the material rests in its function—its ability to enrich the understanding of the issue being considered—in this particular case, human forgiveness.

Another question which might be raised is, What right do I, as one who has agreed to assist Emmie and Tom with their respective presenting problems (depression and feelings of inadequacy), have in interpreting them in terms of the problem with human forgiveness? My response is to point to the importance of thinking of pastoral counseling as operating on several levels at the same time. Emmie and Tom both received help with the issues that they first presented as the problem. Her depression lifted; he became more confident and felt less inadequate with women. Both, however, were invited to see not only their problems, but to discover and rediscover who they were in relation to other persons and to God. The level of the presenting problem— depression or inadequacy—is no less important than the level or dimension of forgiveness. Although many helping relationships have insisted in dealing with human beings in a one-dimensional way, pastoral care and counseling require assisting persons to discover multiple ways of thinking about their lives.

To say to someone at the beginning of pastoral counseling that what I am really interested in—in contrast to what they perceived themselves as wanting—is their learning how to forgive, is not so much inappropriate as it is not understandable. There may be exceptions in the relationships of pastors or spiritual directors to persons whom they have known for many years, but in most relationships one must learn how to talk with another human being about the deeper issues of life. To a young woman who said to me after several months of pastoral counseling, "Why didn't you say when I first came to see you that I was morally and spiritually bankrupt?" I answered, "We hadn't developed a way of talking about that. It takes time to learn how to talk about important and personal things." Speaking too quickly of religious issues tends to undermine their importance.

The use of case material also raises the important question of the relation of a specific case or story to the more general understanding of the issue at hand, in our case, human forgiveness. The more common way of proceeding in such discussions is to move from general principle to specific instance. How, for example, does a Christian understanding of forgiveness inform what Emmie and Tom need to do in relation to those who have wronged them? My use of this case material at this point in the book suggests that I believe the cases of Emmie, Tom, and others can inform the more general Christian understanding of how we forgive those who have injured us. The validation of this position will depend upon whether or not the case material and its accompanying interpretation indeed do this.

Finally, presenting case material inevitably raises the question of confidentiality and respect for the lives of the persons whose stories are used. Obviously, the names of Emmie and Tom and the other persons whose situations I present are fictional, as are a number of the details within each story. They are, therefore, no longer a part of the life of anyone whom I have known. On the other hand, judging by the response which I have received to lectures in which these cases were presented, they are similar enough to the lives of many of us that they seem very much like someone we know. I suspect that we do know them.

The Specialness of Family Relationships

Luke's version of the petition about forgiveness in the Lord's Prayer is, "Forgive us our sins, for we ourselves forgive every one who is indebted to us" (Luke 11:4a). The petition speaks of forgiving everyone, thus stating a general ethical principle. Among those who may be indebted to us and to whom we may be indebted, however, there is a particular kind of indebtedness between us and the members of our immediate family. I recall giving a lecture a number of years ago to a group of retired persons in a noncredit course at a university. I described in some detail a way of thinking about human relations within the family. Throughout the body of my lecture, I noticed that a man on the back row had his eyes closed. When I asked if there were any questions, his eyes popped open and he said to me, somewhat angrily, "That's all theory. I want to know what to do with my son-in-law."

The intensity of that response underscores what I have experienced for years with persons in pastoral counseling. A principle may be accepted as valid and something to be acted upon, but when it is applied to an intense personal relationship, the same person who has accepted that principle intellectually may discover that he or she is finding reasons not to put it into practice. My counselees often do not bother to find reasons. They just don't do it. One way of understanding this problem comes from the field of Christian ethics.

A colleague at Emory University, Richard Bondi, has argued that in the case of special relations, such as those within the family, general princples "do not speak to the wide range of our existence visible in those relations."[1] Or, applied to what I am doing here, there is something in the relationship between Tom and his father, between Emmie and her husband, that cannot adequately be discussed in terms of ethical principles which apply generally to all persons. Our everyday experience tells us that although there are many ways in which these relationships are like all others, there are significant ways in which they are very special and different.

Bondi argues this point by calling attention to what he calls "Outka's dilemma." In his book *Agape: An Ethical Analysis*,[2] Christian ethicist Gene Outka acknowledges that in discussing relationships such as those within the family, one cannot deal only with how those persons are like everyone else because it is what is particular about them that constitutes the relationship. Although Outka has carefully developed the concept of *agape* as a form of justice, his dilemma is that in the case of special relations, general principles may not be adequate to describe the nature of that justice. A principle applied within the context of my relationship to my wife has a different meaning than does the same principle applied in the relationship to a person whom I do not know in this special way.

Ethical principles are usually based upon the assumption that all persons are alike and have a similar rationality, i.e., they can be appealed to in similar ways. What is most characteristic of special relations, however, is the particularities that make them what they are, the histories of those particular persons, and the voluntary obligations they have taken on in relation to those histories. As Bondi puts it, "People are not interchangeable . . . the kind and quality of the special relations I am in help shape the kind of person I am. The 'other' in a special relation . . . is in a real and inescapable sense a part of myself, and I in turn am a part of the other." He goes further to describe "the real specialness of special relations" to be in "the way they reveal some essential characteristics of what it means to be human . . . what they particularly reveal is one of the central paradoxes of human existence: that we are both bound and free." Other relationships do not conceal this, but special relationships make this distinctively human experience painfully clear.

What Bondi calls "the standard account" of how we should live the good life, and this would include our particular concern with human forgiveness, separates "the rational and the affective, the general and the special, the universal and the particular. Part of the paradox of special relations is that they involve us in both sides of those splits, making it impossible for moral theories deriving from one side alone to account for them adequately."[3] Special relations contain obligations and feelings not themselves contained in general principles; therefore, Bondi works out his response to the ethical problem of special relations using the concept of fidelity. As he sees it, fidelity, in contrast to the more familiar concept of covenant, is not a legal bond or principle but a personal commitment to share in a common story with another person. Although the concept applies in a unique way to marriage, it can also be used to interpret other special relations.

Bondi's theory of marriage is a provocative one that has important implications for pastoral care and counseling. My concern here, however, is to underscore from the perspective of another field what I have experienced clinically for many years. When ministers deal with the New Testament question of how many times one should forgive his brother, they are likely to interpret the text so that it applies to the forgiveness of anyone. Forgiving our brother or wife or child, however, is significantly different from forgiving anyone who is not in that special kind of relationship with us. And the answer to that New Testament question, in the light of the concept of special relations, may differ depending upon which brother we are talking about. It depends not only upon principle, but upon the story of our relationship. The ethical principle and the story of that relationship work together dialectically to lead us to an answer to the question.

The issue I am raising is evident for most parents in reflecting upon the difficult-to-impossible problem of trying to be "fair" to their children—applying the family rules dispassionately to each one. The problem is that it is both impossible and inappropriate to be dispassionte. The nature of that special relationship is that it involves both reason and passion. The story of the relationship and of the family is involved in the application of the principle. This is true of the case material presented earlier in the chapter, i.e., the relationship between Emmie and her husband and the relationship between Tom and his father. The issue of the special relations involved affects the application of any ethical principle concerning human forgiveness.

What I attempt to do now, however, is to discuss these special relationships in terms of psychological theory in order that some of the issues evident in this brief discussion of ethical theory may be clarified psychologically. The psychological literature on these two relationships is so immense that the choice of theoretical resources to interpret their specialness will necessarily seem arbitrary. Again, however, I turn to my own experience and reflect upon what has been most useful in assisting me to interpret it. The psychological writers whose views of relationships within the family seem most to argue for their specialness are Ivan Boszormenyi-Nagy and Carl Whitaker. Both are viewed as authorities within the field of family therapy but in many ways appear to be saying diametrically opposite things about family relationships. They say them, however, with equal strength and conviction, and the fact that they argue for the special character of family relationships in such different ways seems to me to emphasize that specialness more effectively. Their differences also seem to illustrate the dialectical tension in special relationships between the justice that Nagy seeks in his work with families, and the irrationality and impossibility emphasized by Whitaker.

The Special Relationship of Parent and Child

I once said to Ivan Nagy, after hearing one of his presentations on family therapy, that I felt a little like I had been in an Old Testament class. He seemed a bit disturbed by this and insisted that what he meant by ethics and ethical balance were not based upon any religion. I was in no position to argue about the basis of his theory—although I still had my suspicions—but Nagy's views give powerful support to the importance accorded the family by the Judeo-Christian tradition.

Nagy feels that what some therapists interpret as an abnormal concern for one's family of origin is in fact a natural kind of family loyalty which is normative for everyone and dangerous to ignore. This loyalty, he believes, is a powerful part of the unconscious. "Until the Post-Victorian age," Nagy insists, "the issues of family loyalty were largely unformulated because they were taken for granted. Our age, on the other hand, denies these issues with the help of the myths of individual material success and endless struggle against the threat of authority." He sees social fragmentaion as making it appear as if loyalty were not operative in today's family, but under those conditions issues of loyalty simply "arise surreptitiously and unexpectedly." There is within the family a "multipersonal loyalty fabric" which, according to Nagy, "implies the existence of structured group expectations to which all members are committed. In this sense loyalty pertains to what Buber called 'the order of the human world.' "[4] To understand a family, nothing is more important than to know who are bound together in loyalty and what loyalty means to each of them.

"Each person maintains a bookkeeping of his perception of the balances of past, present, and future give-and-take. What has been 'invested' into the system and what has been withdrawn in the form of support received or one's exploitive use of others remains written into the invisible account of obligations." Nagy notes that through the course of life vertical loyalty commitments clash with horizontal ones. What is required is a flexibilty that incorporates the new loyalty toward one's mate and children into the existing fabric of the larger family system. Adjustment is not a final resolution; it is a closing of a previous phase and a continuing tension to rebalance old but surviving expectations with new ones.

The concept necessary for describing the balance in the family loyalty system is justice. "Justice," he says, "can be regarded as a web of invisible fibers running through the length and width of the history of family relationships, holding the system in social equilibrium throughout phases of physical togetherness and separation." Nothing is more significant in determining the relationship between a parent and a child than the degree of fairness expected in their interactions with each other. Moreover, "the traditional framework for assessing justice among adults fails as a guideline when it comes to the balance of the parent-child relationship." In the family there is a "transgenerational bookkeeping of merits . . . which cannot be objectively quantified as material benefits can be."

This bookkeeping system involves what Nagy calls "the ledger of justice which resides in the interpersonal fabric of human order" or Martin Buber's "realm of the between." A major complication of the ledger in interpersonal family accounting is that it seems to operate in terms of quantifiable concepts, such as power, wealth, and domination; but in the personal sphere of the family, those with little in the way of these obvious resources can exert great influence in the way the ledger operates. Moreover, a family ledger must be "audited" for meaning because the concepts do not remain fixed. Ideally, or in more healthy families, there is a lively "economy" of giving and receiving among the members of the system with the level of activity understood to be more important than "the bottom line."

Nagy illustrates how the ledger operates in the family system with the case of a woman who tells her husband, "You have taken advantage of me all my life." The slip of the tongue, he says, is significant. This woman's injured sense of justice has become overwhelming and unjustly accusatory. Her mother "has always regarded her as ungrateful and made her feel guilty over anything she has ever done." Since this matter is "unnegotiable between her mother and herself," she has sought a balancing of her "account" through her husband and acts as if her husband were accountable for her lifelong relationship with her mother. Her husband states: "When I begin to point out that she is messy, neglects housekeeping, etc., she retorts that I don't have a clean slate either."[5]

The major issue in sorting out parent-child relationships in our time, according to Nagy, is justice within, minimally, a three-generational context. What remained unbalanced in one generation is expected to be balanced in the next. What is often overtly "ignored and denied is the parents' deeply felt conviction about their right to expect from their child gratitude and at least a limited repayment of their ministrations."

In terms of the child's expectations from his or her parents, Nagy suggests that if the parents remain in arrears to the child in performing their parental obligations, the child will tend to treat the whole world as untrustworthy and see all people as debtors. "The actual unsettled merit balance begets the basic formula for mistrust," and the child develops a paranoid orientation to life where the whole world is "in arrears."

The therapeutic effort toward rebalancing familial accounts involves, among other things, rehabilitating family members' painful and shameful images of their parents. "We have not," Nagy says, "seen anyone benefit from a therapeutic outcome in which a person only faces, realizes, and expresses his contempt and disaffection towards his parents. In our experience this is a losing game for everyone concerned." Therapy involves each family member's exploring his or her developmental past which, in effect, allows other members to understand and experience him or her as a person, not just as a parent, mother, or wife. It attempts to facilitate the discovery of the other's common humanness, or—as Harry Stack Sullivan, whose theories of the forties contributed to the family therapy of the sixties, might have put it—how family members are "more alike than otherwise." Such a discovery, in Nagy's terms, moves toward rebalancing the ledger.

What is most pathological in a family, however, is not so much an unbalanced ledger as a fixed, unchangeable balance.[6] The balance within all families is at times unfair and destructive to one or more of its members. That is a fact of the contingencies and choices of life. An openness to examining the whole family system and interpersonally adjusting the account balances as needed is, perhaps, the family's most important responsibility to itself.

To me, the values Nagy embraces and advocates are more striking than his theory of family psychotherapy. He affirms the special and inescapable nature of the parent-child and child-parent relationships in a world which he sees as tending to look at all relationships as if they were the same. It is the nature of family members to insist on balance and fairness when all evidence seems to point the other way. Moreover, there is no such thing as a one- or two-generation family. All of us live with at least three-generational assumptions. Not only can you go home again, you must. Jacob must seek the blessing from Isaac whatever the cost.

Nagy's work helps us to understand why forgiveness in the parent-child and child-parent relationships is so important, why the rage at personal injury is so intense, and why the defenses erected to prevent further injury are so powerful. His use of Buber to assert the relational nature of humankind seems appropriate, as is his using the analogy of the I-It and the I-Thou relationships to underscore the differences between the objective and subjective worlds of experience. The identification of the I-Thou relationship with what family relationships should be seems to me, however, to be both an inappropriate use of Buber and one which is inconsistent with Nagy's own major emphasis. On the one hand, I-Thou is an existential category which affirms the possibility of intensity and intimacy in particular, but often isolated, moments. The family's invisible loyalties, on the other hand, are not momentary experiences but structural conditions. They express the continuity of relationships more than their quality. Nevertheless, although one might criticize various elements of his theory, Nagy offers one of the most powerful affirmations of the specialness of family relationships that can be found in the literature.

I move now to discuss some of the ways in which the relationship of husband and wife is special. Although the nature of that relationship is inescapably related to the parent-child relationships of each spouse's family of origin, and these play themselves out in the marital relationship in a variety of ways, there are unique elements in marital specialness which also must be taken into account.

The Special Relationship of Husband and Wife

Whereas Ivan Nagy discusses family relationships in terms of loyalty, justice, and balance, Carl Whitaker seems to address them in a diametrically opposite way. The contrast between Nagy and Whitaker is quickly evident in this statement on assumptions about marriage:

We assume that the usual rules of human social behavior do not apply to marriage nor to other intimate relationships. . . . Dr. Warkentin has a wonderful quote: "All's fair in love and war and marriage is both." . . . consistency is impossible in feeling relationships. Woe be to the therapist who tries to be consistent; the only thing worse is a parent who tries to be consistent. Furthermore, such considerations as decency, face saving, factual honesty are all of minor significance in marriage.[7]

The comment by his editors that few therapists view marriage as important for human development as does Carl Whitaker seems quite consistent with what I have learned of him through personal acquaintance with some of his former colleagues. The apparently radical difference between Whitaker and Nagy comes not only in the contrast of Whitaker's essentially oral style with Nagy's carefully written one, but also from Whitaker's conviction that the intimacy which is the essential quality of marriage can only be described irrationally. The unmarried person for him is a biological cripple, unable to reproduce himself or herself and one who is psychologically incomplete as well. Humankind's incompleteness causes a yearning for communion and closeness, and marriage serves as the most valuable form of experiencing this closeness. "People are good for each other," says Whitaker, "according to the degree to which they are intimate together."

Arguing for the difference of the marital relationship from other relationships, he identifies two types of relational problems. One is exemplified in the person who relates to his or her spouse as if marriage were a relationship like all others: the salesman, for example, who can't understand why his usually effective techniques of persuasion don't work on his wife. He observes that she doesn't behave like everyone else and seems confused by this. Another type of relational problem is exemplified by the schizophrenic who "has a private relations system with everybody. He wants to have the kind of intimacy—the unconscious to unconscious relationship with the guy he meets on the street and has just said hello to."[8] This may also be seen in persons who are not so obviously disturbed as the schizophrenic, but who feel that their religion requires them to be personal with everyone. The intimate relationship of marriage can never be just like other relationships, nor can other relationships have the kind of intimacy that marriage has. Whitaker, in his own way, has said something very close to what Buber describes in his discussion of I-It and I-Thou, but with more practical than philosophical concerns.

Most American marriages, he says, are "pseudo-therapeutic" in that we unconsciously find people who can help or complement us and to whom we can give something. This kind of marital choice is not pathological. It simply illustrates the power of the unconscious and the wisdom of marital choice. One's marital choice is not something that one can quickly turn away from in order to escape one's problems. A marriage for Whitaker—following Freud afar off—must be sexual and aggressive in order to be alive. The marriage relationship is special also because it has a significant time dimension. One of its functions is "to increase the rate of metabolism." It does this at particular moments, but also in a more general sense. "I suppose that nobody lives as hot a life if they aren't married" because marriage, according to Whitaker, functions as a precipitator of stress, an increase in anxiety, and an increase in affect, both negative and positive. This is "one of its great contributions."

> It also precipitates creativity, and not just biologically, but in a general sense, and it does this by disturbing the homeostasis, by disrupting the individual's organization, his solidity, his quieting down. It's more difficult to burn out at 25 if you suddenly find yourself a mate, and you settle into a permanent battle as to who's going to do what to whom with whose gun.[9]

Although Whitaker's colloquial style does not lend itself to clarity and consistency in presentation, what he says in his informal way emhasizes the specialness of the marriage relationship more convincingly than does the writing of most religious writers. Note, for example, the "high view" of marriage implicit in the paradoxical way in which he describes how increased closeness facilitates separateness.

> This is a weird kind of business, but the closer they get, the more separate they are. If they don't grow separate, they can't grow closer. If they can't increase their individuality, they can't increase their oneness. . . . The more you are free to be with others, your wife specifically, significant others, the more you are free to be with yourself.[10]

Or, finally, Whitaker's description of the specialness of his own home may be an even better way to state the closeness-separateness irony.

> My home is . . . the arena for the struggle involved in my most special partnership, the ebb and flow, the fluctuation, the freedom for greater closeness and thereby, for greater separation. The anxiety in the change of direction, either toward or away from my wife, is what makes the sparks and what keeps home like a sauna bath or the snow plunge. It's that exciting segment of the day that keeps me alive.[11]

Since my concern here is not to discuss marriage or family therapy, but only to present Whitaker's view of the marriage relationship, what I have presented may be enough to convey his point of view. Arguing in a radically different way from Nagy, Whitaker—with Nagy—insists that relationships within the family have a special quality. They cannot simply be included in a general theory of human relationships. Although one cannot identify family relationships with I-Thou in contrast to the I-It of other relationships, one can say that their difference from other relationships is as different as the personal relation of I-Thou is to the more impersonal and social relationship of I-It.

My experience as a pastoral counselor tells me that there is something particularly difficult in forgiving one's husband, wife, parent, or child—those who are in special relation to us. The discussion of these relationships from the point of view of the writers whom we considered in this chapter has suggested some of the reasons for that. These special relationships are so intense and have so many features peculiar to the history of that particular relationship that they do not fit neatly into a general theory about how persons ought to treat one another. This is not to say that general principles—including whatever Christians say about forgiveness—do not apply to them. It is to say, however, that in applying such principles invisible loyalties, irrational expectations, and other factors related to the peculiar character of family relationships must be taken into account.

In the case of Emmie, for example, forgiving Elmer requires some satisfaction to her sense of justice. Simply trying to convince her that bitterness was not good for her and that forgiveness was better, although true, would not do that. Providing care for Emmie involved taking into account not only his leaving her for another woman and any other acts of unfaithfulness, but also the nature of Emmie's faithfulness to her parents and her expectations of her children's faithfulness to her. It is, as Nagy has suggested, at least a three-generational issue. To have ongoing meaning, any act of forgiveness cannot stand alone, but must be consistent with Emmie's part in her ongoing family history. In her situation, before any check written for forgiveness could be cashed, there were old accounts to be balanced and emotional losses to be compensated for. Pastors need to be more aware of this kind of thing as they deal with situations involving human forgiveness.

One thing should be evident at this point in the discussion. Forgiving a parent or a mate involves a good deal more than the application of a Christian principle about forgiveness. Moreover, the commonly accepted view that there is greater virtue in the harder one tries to forgive is also suspect—at least for the special relations of the family. One is tempted to look for a quick resolution to the problem of human forgiveness in that solution to all problems taught to Georgians by our former governor, Lester Maddox, who once commented that "what our prison system needs is a better quality of prisoner." The problem with human forgiveness is considerably more complicated than finding a better quality of Christian.

The question we are left with at the end of this chapter is, In what ways does the answer to the New Testament question, How often should I forgive my brother? apply to the actual and the symbolic brother? To what extent does any general principle of Christian response to another apply to the special relations within a family? Such relations are different and contribute to there being a problem with human forgiveness, but what changes do those relationships make in the application of principle to these special cases? The other side of the question is, To what extent do issues involved in special relationships affect relationships to those who are not in special relation to us? These questions I leave until later in order to move on to the powerful experience which consistently obstructs human forgiveness—particularly in special relationships—the experience of shame.

Notes

1. Richard Bondi, *Fidelity and the Good Life: Special Relations in Christian Ethics* (Ann Arbor: Xerox University Microfilms, 1981), p. 38.

2. Gene Outka, *Agape: An Ethical Analysis* (New Haven: Yale University Press, 1972).

3. Bondi, *Fidelity and the Good Life*, pp. 38-39, 43, 44.

4. Ivan Boszormenyi-Nagy and Geraldine M. Spark, *Invisible Loyalties: Reciprocity in Intergenerational Family Therapy* (New York: Harper & Row, 1973), pp. 149, 37.

5. Ibid., pp. 39-40, 54, 55, 65-66.

6. Ibid., pp. 86, 91, 95, 101.

7. Carl Whitaker, *From Psyche to System: The Evolving Therapy of Carl Whitaker*, ed. John R. Neill and David P. Kniskern (New York and London: The Guilford Press, 1982), p. 187.

8. Ibid., pp. 164, 165, 168.

9. Ibid., p. 171.

10. Ibid., p. 172.

11. Carl Whitaker, "Sauna Bath and Snow Plunge," *Voices: The Art and Science of Psychotherapy*, vol. 2, no. 1, p. 33.

Shame and the Problem
of Human Forgiveness

F orgive us our sins—*for we acknowledge our*
shame that we may recognize our guilt.

Shame must be understood before human forgiveness can be understood. The pastoral counselor who is to assist persons in their problem with forgiving must be very familiar with the function of shame in human life. Christian theology and tradition have obscured this fact by the close association of forgiveness with guilt. Thus human forgiveness has been assumed to be concerned with specific sins and specific actions, whereas it is much more a problem of the shame and the vulnerability of the whole self. Both Emmie and Tom, for example, felt more sinned against than sinner. Pastoral counseling involved helping them acknowledge and share the shame of rejection and feelings of inadequacy before guilt and forgiveness could actually be relevant. Guilt can more nearly be dealt with according to rational principle, whereas shame is inevitably relational and personal.

The pastoral concern with guilt has led to an overemphasis on catharsis and confession, often at the expense of the slow development of an empathic relationship in which shame could be expressed. This chapter, therefore, is an extensive examination of the experience of shame, so extensive perhaps that the reader may feel that I have deviated from my central concern with forgiveness. What I am attempting to do, however, is to argue that the experience of shame is the context for dealing with human forgiveness and that a thorough understanding of shame is essential for doing pastoral counseling today.

Both the dictionaries that I have in my study use the term *guilt* to define the meaning of *shame*, but do not use *shame* to define *guilt*. According to the *Funk and Wagnalls Standard Dictionary*, for example, shame is "a painful sense of guilt or degradation caused by consciousness of guilt or of anything degrading, unworthy or immodest." The second meaning is given as "a restraining sense of pride, decency or modesty."[1] Carl Schneider has described the first meaning of shame as *disgrace* shame and the second meaning, *discretion* shame. Disgrace shame comes after whatever has been done that is shameful. Discretion shame, as the dictionary definition suggests, involves the restraint which may prevent the shaming of oneself, another person, or the larger society.

Our society, according to Schneider, thinks of shame primarily in terms of disgrace shame and therefore "fails to understand the significant role as a positive restraining influence that the sense of shame—as modesty or discretion—plays in human experience." Disgrace shame clearly seems to be an affect, but discretion shame is more difficult to limit and locate. "The concept of *shamelessness* suggests that the lack of a proper sense of shame is a moral deficiency and that the possession of a sense of shame is a moral obligation." Discretion shame "not only reflects, but sustains, our personal and social ordering of the world." It "recognizes what is the proper attitude, the fitting response." To be an appropriate member of society, one must possess the proper degree of discretion shame.[2] Disgrace shame, on the other hand,

> is a painful experience of the disintegration of one's world. A break occurs in the self's relationship with itself and/or others. An awkward, uncomfortable space opens up in the world. The self is no longer whole, but divided. It feels less than it wants to be, less than at its best it knows itself to be.[3]

Most of what we discuss in this chapter is disgrace shame, but both types of shame are closely related in that they involve experiences of the self in relationship. In his exposition, Schneider makes use of Jean-Paul Sartre, a major contributor to the phenomenology of shame to emphasize shame's relational nature. In shame there is an "apprehension of something and this something is *me*. I am ashamed of what I *am*. Shame therefore realizes an intimate relation of myself to myself. . . . Shame is by nature recognition, I recognize that I am as the Other sees me." Although disgrace shame is painful and disorienting, a more sustained look, says Schneider, "reveals an underlying core of positive belief and self-valuation . . . shame implies that a person cares." He quotes Paul Pruyser's observation that shame has the seeds of betterment in it. "It is future-directed and lives from hope."[4]

I am convinced that a thorough understanding of shame is essential not only to deal with the problem of human forgiveness but also for the total work of pastoral care today. The psychological view of shame which seems to me to be most relevant for the pastoral counselor is Heinz Kohut's. I discuss that theory in some detail toward the end of the chapter. Since, however, the relation between shame and guilt has been inadequately discussed in the literature of pastoral counseling,[5] it seems important to me to present a survey of some of the more important views of shame and guilt that preceded Kohut.

Biblical Perspectives on Shame and Guilt

In the Bible, shame is understood both objectively and subjectively.[6] Objectively, it may be the disgrace a sinner brings upon himself or herself (Lev. 20:17), or it may be the result of natural calamities such as barrenness (Gen. 30:23). It is sometimes viewed as divine judgment upon sinners (Ps. 44:9). A frequent Old Testament expression is "to be put to shame" (Isa. 54:4). "Subjectively, shame is experienced as guilt for sin'"[7] (and here note the identification of shame and guilt or at least the failure to distinguish between them, Jer.

2:26), as a violation of one's honor and modesty (I Cor. 11:6), or simply as a result of disappointment (Hos. 10:6). In the New Testament, shame is not a frequent topic other than in quotations from other sources. The term is used in relation to the cross of Christ, but in general the New Testament seems to have little time for shame other than to note that Christian hope never puts a man to shame by failing or deceiving him (Rom. 5:5).

Pedersen's classic study of the life and culture of Israel views shame as not having blessing. "Trouble, misery and misfortune, like hunger, are in themselves a shame" (Ezek. 36:30). The source of shame is weakness, usually weakness in battle. Defeat "deprives the soul of its worth and shakes its self-confidence. . . . Where honour is the absolute maintenance of self, there shame must consist in being unable to maintain oneself." Nevertheless, Pedersen insists, "through prophets and psalms constantly rings the confidence that Yahweh will not let his faithful suffer shame."[8]

Lyn Bechtel Huber, in a recent dissertation study of shame in the Old Testament, notes that there has been surprisingly little examination of a biblical understanding of shame and suggests that this lack of research may be related to the "general guilt-orientation of Western society. . . . Most people function with a more pronounced guilt-sensitivity than shame-sensitivity, and this makes it more difficult to be aware of shame. . . . This guilt-orientation," she continues, "is often thought to stem from Judeo-Christian religious beliefs and traditions, but we have found that within the Old Testament shame is not subsumed under guilt in this way . . . a strong guilt-orientation and emphasis on a 'guilty conscience' are characteristic of Western society and not of biblical society."[9]

In her study, Huber found that "Hebrew shame vocabulary does not contain an inherent meaning of guilt. . . . Linguistically there seems to be no connection in Hebrew between shame and guilt, although contextually they can sometimes be interrelated." In defining the emotional experience of shame from the point of view of ancient Israel, Huber found shame strongly related to pride. Shame arises when pride has been violated, when people have become aware of their failure to achieve and have feelings of inferiority, insignificance, inadequacy, and unacceptability. Because shame involves these powerful feelings, it is viewed in the Old Testament as contributing to the breaking down of self-sufficiency and increasing reliance upon God. The doctrine of Israel's election is a theological response to the feelings of inadequacy associated with shame. "Election is an essential balance to shame/shaming that allows the shamed person to have confidence in his ultimate acceptance and to turn to God for face-saving revenge to remove his sense of shame."[10]

With respect to the experience of shame as it appears in the Bible, the passage of scripture that has had the most influence upon Christian belief is the Yahwist presentation of the story of the Fall in Genesis 3. I present some of the insights of only three of the many interpreters, and my choices are in many ways arbitrary. Dietrich Bonhoeffer interprets the story both in his *Ethics* and in his lectures on the first chapters of Genesis. Viewing the story theologically, he comments that "instead of seeing God man sees himself." He "perceives himself in his disunion with God and with men. He perceives that he is naked. Lacking the protection, the covering, which God and his fellow-man afforded him, he finds himself laid bare. Hence there arises shame."[11]

Shame, for Bonhoeffer, at its most profound level, is humankind's grief over its estrangement from God. This is theological affirmation more than biblical interpretation. When he talks about what this feels like, however, Bonhoeffer gets into the psychological dimension of this theologically described state. Shame is primarily related not to being at fault or to guilt but to lacking something. Being seen by another is a reminder of the lost wholeness of life. "Shame is more original than remorse." It may arise "whenever there is experience of man's disunion," and the condition of humankind is such that it longs "for the restoration of the lost unity."

> Shame can be overcome only when the original unity is restored, when man is once again clothed by God in the other man. . . . Shame is overcome only in the enduring of an act of final shaming, namely the becoming manifest of knowledge before God. . . . Shame is overcome only in the shaming through the forgiveness of sin, that is to say through the restoration of fellowship with God and men.[12]

The answer to shame, for Bonhoeffer, is reunion and fellowship. Under the conditions of human existence, however, men and women live in a state of covering and discovering, between self-concealment and self-revelation, and this is what must be addressed when we deal with shame.

Claus Westermann's interpretation of Genesis 3 is also theological, but Westermann emphasizes the psychological even more than Bonhoeffer does. In good sermonic fashion he notes that "the narrative portrays three events: the opening of their eyes, the awareness, the covering." Humankind's condition of other-awareness—knowledge and awakening from naïveté—is bought at the cost of painful self-awareness and shame. The aprons, the defense against nakedness, were an ineffective attempt to deal with shame. In fact, humankind's shame is uncoverable, but interestingly, the struggle to cover that shame has a positive dimension in the creativity and color of the defenses that make up at least part of what we view as civilization.[13]

Gerhard von Rad's interpretation also reflects the richness of this powerful and primitive human story. I do not know to what psychological theory von Rad is indebted, but it is clear that in his exposition he is making psychological assumptions about the relation between shame and guilt as well as about the nature of the human self. As he interprets the story, Adam and Eve react to having taken the forbidden fruit "not primarily with a spiritual feeling of guilt, but with bodily shame. . . . Shame, for our narrator," he continues, "is the most elementary emotion of a guilty feeling at the deepest root of human existence, the sign of a breach that reaches to the lowest level of our physical being."

[44]

Note the entanglement of guilt and shame in von Rad's interpretation, as he sees guilt as the primary category with shame described as an emotion associated with our physical being and touching the "deepest root of human existence." He uses Emil Brunner's theology to suggest further that humankind's grasp for the forbidden "tears apart body and spirit" and that the reaction to this innermost disturbance is the feeling of shame. To appear naked before God was an abomination for ancient Israel. In the cult every form of bodily exposure was carefully guarded against (Exod. 20:26). If shame was the sign of a disturbance in man's relation to other men, then fear before God was the sign of a disorder in his relation to his Creator. Fear and shame are henceforth the incurable stigmata of the Fall in man.

Humankind's first response to God involves emotions "which exist objectively and not yet consciously, completely beyond and before any rational reflection." In the second answer to the questioning God, von Rad continues, "something new appears. Now begins the intellectual wrestle with guilt . . . and with its assistance man tries to clear himself of guilt."[14] In this interpretation of primary human experience, shame and guilt are closely connected, with shame occurring first and being associated with the body, with emotions, and with the split between body and spirit. Guilt, however, is viewed as the dominant category of which shame is a part. It is also associated with the intellect and seems to be something which we human beings move to as seemingly more manageable than the experience of shame.

These expositions of the biblical story all involve psychological interpretion. Von Rad particularly suggests the way in which both Christian theology and ministry may have de-emphasized shame in order to emphasize guilt. That has been the concern of modern psychology as well, and it provides good reason to explore the explicitly psychological theories about self, shame, and guilt. Keep in mind, however, that my concern in presenting psychological theory is not so much with the theory itself, but to clarify some of the psychological issues in pastoral counseling with persons like Emmie and Tom. How can we best respond to their shame and guilt and thus help them with the problem of human forgiveness?

What Shame and Guilt Feel Like

Franz Alexander was one of the early writers on the phenomenology of shame. Although he seldom used the term, the phenomena he describes in terms of feelings of inferiority are an important part of what is referred to in this chapter as *shame*. Alexander sees both guilt and inferiority feelings as growing out of the tension between what I am and what I aspire to be. Guilt, he says, is always felt as "a pressure, as an unpleasant tension, the expectation of an impending evil, of a deserved punishment." It is an internal reaction to one's own hostile tendencies rather than to an external threat. The psychological content of guilt feelings, according to Alexander, is something like this: "I am not good. What I want to do (or what I did) is mean or low. I deserve contempt and punishment." A sense of justice violated must be present for there to be guilt feelings; thus, "the most severe guilt feelings develop in sons of loving, understanding, and mild fathers who do not give any justification for hostile feelings."

Whereas guilt feelings have an inhibiting effect upon the expression of hostility because of the introjected sense of justice, inferiority feelings have just the opposite effect. Feelings of inadequacy are not connected with any sense of justice, but with being weak, inefficient, and unable to accomplish something. Rather than inhibiting aggression, they stimulate it, sometimes against someone who has no fault other than being stronger than oneself. "Shame" (and this is one of the few places in the article that Alexander specifically relates shame and inferiority) "for being licked by Bob stimulates hostile competition and ambition, or will lead to an attempt to depreciate Bob."[15]

Alexander insists that guilt and inferiority are "two entirely different emotions." Inferiority feelings are

presocial phenomena, whereas guilt feelings are results of social adjustment. It is noteworthy that under the pressure

[46]

of guilty conscience the human being may assume such an amount of inhibition and may be driven so far back towards a dependent and help-seeking attitude that it becomes incompatible with his narcissism. To remedy this narcissistic injury caused by very strong dependence, he may recourse to extreme forms of independent and aggressive behavior. In this way social inhibitions may become the very source of nonsocial behavior.[16]

Later on I discuss in more detail the meaning of "narcissistic injury" in connection with the self-psychology of Heinz Kohut. At this point it may simply be understood as injury to one's self.

Probably the most familiar psychological theory having to do with shame and guilt is that of Erik Erikson, who related shame to the second of his developmental stages and guilt to the third. "Shame," says Erikson, "is an emotion insufficiently studied, because in our civilization it is so early and easily absorbed by guilt." This statement suggests the point of view of this chapter that the merging of shame into guilt is a significant part of the problem of human forgiveness. I quote at length from Erikson because what he says quickly reminds us of what shame feels like:

> Shame supposes that one is completely exposed and conscious of being looked at: in one word, self-conscious. One is visible and not ready to be visible; which is why we dream of shame as a situation in which we are stared at in a condition of incomplete dress, in night attire, "with one's pants down." Shame is early expressed in an impulse to bury one's face, or to sink, right then and there, into the ground. But this, I think, is essentially rage turned against the self. He who is ashamed would like to force the world not to look at him, not to notice his exposure. He would like to destroy the eyes of the world. Instead he must wish for his own invisibility. This potentiality is abundantly used in the educational method of "shaming" used so exclusively by some primitive peoples. Visual shame precedes auditory guilt, which is a sense of badness to be had all by oneself when nobody watches and when everything is quiet—except the voice of the superego. Such shame exploits an increasing sense of being small, which can develop only as the child stands up and as his awareness permits him to note the relative measures of size and power.[17]

[47]

Silvan Tomkins's 1963 study of affects also offers a vivid description of shame. He believes that shame, shyness, and guilt are one emotion served by the same neurophysiological mechanisms. Consciously, however, they are quite different phenomena. Shame involves the experience of indignity, defeat, and alienation.

> Though terror speaks to life and death and distress makes of the world a vale of tears, yet shame strikes deepest into the heart of man. While terror and distress hurt, they are wounds inflicted from outside which penetrate the smooth surface of the ego; but shame is felt as an inner torment, a sickness of the soul. It does not matter whether the humiliated one has been shamed by derisive laughter, or whether he mocks himself. In either event he feels himself naked, defeated, alienated, lacking in dignity and worth.[18]

Helen B. Lewis notes that although the many varieties of shame—mortification, humiliation, embarrassment, feeling ridiculous, chagrin, shyness, and modesty—represent different psychological states, they all involve the "other" as referent. Mortification involves a relatively distant relationship to the other and has an element of wounded pride. Humiliation, however, is experienced as shifting rapidly back and forth between seeing oneself from the point of view of the other and from the point of view of the self. Embarrassment involves primarily the loss of one's powers in relation to the other.[19]

In comparing the type of thought that differentiates shame and guilt, Lewis describes the guilty thought process as follows:

> How could I have *done that;* what an injurious *thing* to have done; how I *hurt so-and-so;* what a moral lapse that *act* was; what will become of *that* or *him,* now that I have neglected to do it, or injured him. How sould I be *punished* to *make amends?*

The thought process for shame, in contrast, is something like this:

> How could *I* have done that; what an *idiot I am*—how humiliating; what a *fool,* what an *uncontrolled person*—how

[48]

mortifying; how unlike so-and-so, who does not do such things; how *awful and worthless I am.*

Part of the power of shame is that it can keep ideas of guilt and feelings of shame active even after appropriate amends have been made. Shame has the potential for a wide range of connections between particular transgressions and failures of the self through a process which in psychological theory is called "stimulus generalization." Shame for a defeat or a rejection, for example, evokes guilt for transgression. Thus shame and guilt are easily confused by the experiencing person and tend to stay entangled with each other.[20]

I am discussing what shame and guilt feel like from the point of view of these psychological theorists for the very practical reason of interpreting and clarifying what has appeared to me to be the experience of Emmie and Tom and many other parishioners, patients, and counselees. In Emmie there appeared to be an overriding experience of shame at her rejection by her husband which was unmixed with guilt, except perhaps the denial of any guilt on her part. The shame, of course, was such a powerful experience that in the beginning of our relationship it was not expressed. What was expressed were symptoms of depression and then anger. In the course of pastoral counseling, the shame precipitated by her husband's action was gradually expressed and related to other powerful experiences of shame and inferiority that occurred in Emmie's family of origin.

In Tom's counseling with me, shame and guilt were entangled from the beginning in ways similar to those described above. Tom felt inferior to his father and inadequate to the tasks left to him through his parents' divorce. Because his father was so loving and understanding, however, any anger and resentment Tom felt were quickly replaced by guilt. Thus, in contrast to Emmie, who at first denied her guilt, Tom experienced both shame and guilt in a very powerful way. Before exploring these phenomena further, however, it seems important to examine some of the ways in which shame and guilt can be differentiated theoretically.

Theoretical Differences Between Shame and Guilt

The theoretical treatment of shame and guilt most frequently cited in literature is the 1953 work of Gerhart Piers and Milton B. Singer, *Shame and Guilt: A Psychoanalytic and a Cultural Study.* They note that "only Erikson and Alexander ascribe to shame an importance equal to 'guilt' in human pathology" and in their own attempt to emphasize shame's importance differentiate between the two concepts at four points:

> 1) Shame arises out of a tension between the ego and the ego ideal, not between ego and superego as in guilt,
>
> 2) Whereas guilt is generated whenever a boundary (set by the superego) is touched or transgressed, shame occurs when a goal (presented by the ego ideal) is not being reached. It thus indicates a real "shortcoming." Guilt anxiety accompanies transgression; shame, failure.
>
> 3) The unconscious, irrational threat implied in shame anxiety is abandonment, and not mutilation (castration) as in guilt.
>
> 4) The Law of Talion does not obtain in the development of shame, as it generally does in guilt.[21]

In psychoanalytic theory the superego is concerned with moral transgressions and with reactions to failure of nonmoral strivings, such as the failure of one's powers to accomplish a particular purpose. The superego "groups together all the occasions when the person is evaluating himself, either positively or negatively, and whether the context for self-evaluation is moral or nonmoral" because of the "common psychological properties of the self-evaluating function."[22] Shame and guilt may also occur sequentially or as defenses against each other. As Helen Lewis points out, one may "feel ashamed of some failure in achievement and in the next moment feel guilty for caring about success. Or one may feel guilty for some moral lapse and remain ashamed of 'moral weakness' long after the specific lapse has been forgotten."[23] Moreover, some of the self-evaluative

SHAME AND THE PROBLEM OF HUMAN FORGIVENESS

function may take place outside awareness. A person may, for example, be pleased with himself or herself for feeling guilty and be unaware of the process which brought that feeling of pleasure.

A recent study by Gershen Kaufman makes use of the interpersonal psychiatry of Harry Stack Sullivan and the object relations theories of British psychiatrists Fairbairn and Guntrip to discuss shame interpersonally rather than psychodynamically. Shame, he says, is likely whenever our most basic expectations of a significant other are suddenly exposed as wrong. To have someone we value unexpectedly betray our trust opens the self inside of us and exposes it to view. "What a fool I was to trust him!" How familiar that reaction is! The anger evidenced is but a mask covering the ruptured self.[24]

Few strivings, according to Kaufman, are as compelling as the need to identify with someone, to feel a part of something, or to belong somewhere. "So powerful is that striving that we might feel obliged to do most anything in order to secure our place." Identification begins within the family as the young child models himself or herself after one or both parents. "No wish is stronger than to be like the beloved or needed parent."

> We internalize, literally take inside, mainly through identification. Specific ways of thinking and feeling about ourselves are learned in relationship with significant others, parents most especially, but including anyone who becomes important to us.[25]

Through identification, not only the child but persons at all stages in life internalize specific ways of thinking and feeling about themselves, ways in which they are treated by significant others, and images of who they are. When these feelings, behaviors, and images involve deficient worth as a person, the interpersonal experience of being shamed, intentionally or unintentionally, by another has been internalized. The internalization of shame means that shame is not simply one feeling among many which may become activated at various times and then pass on.

[51]

"Rather, internalized shame is now experienced as a deep abiding sense of being defective, never quite good enough as a person. It forms the foundation around which other feelings about the self will be experienced." It may also be activated at any time without interpersonal stimulus.

Another consequence of the internalization of shame is what Kaufman calls the "internal shame spiral." A triggering event occurs, and the person is suddenly enmeshed in shame. The experience becomes totally internal, frequently with visual imagery present.

> The shame feelings and thoughts flow in a circle endlessly triggering each other. The precipitating event is relived internally over and over, causing the sense of shame to deepen, to absorb other neutral experiences that happened before as well as those that may come later, until finally the self is engulfed. In this way, shame becomes paralyzing.[26]

Kaufman emphasizes the alienating function of shame by pointing out that shame "can altogether sever one's essential human ties." The person may feel forced to renounce the very striving to belong itself and resignedly accept an alienated existence. No matter how strong his or her inner yearning to belong may be, dignity as a human being matters more; and a shamed person may withdraw from a relationship in order to maintain that dignity.[27]

Tom's shame, for example, is evident in his sense of not quite being good enough in relation to his father. He feels guilt for his anger toward his father for leaving him and all that resulted from it, but the stronger feeling is the shame of not quite measuring up. It is expressed occasionally in his impotence, but more often—in spite of impressive evidence of his success in most of his endeavors—in the feeling of being a boy in a man's world. With Emmie, the initial shame at rejection by Elmer was soon associated in her counseling with her shame in relation to her mother and all that her mother represented. This was accentuated by the event of her mother's death during the time Emmie was in counseling. In her grief, shame and anger were also evident, although the anger was intense and generalized enough that it covered her shame most of the time. What seemed to be underlying it was a powerful sense of inadequacy in relation to her mother's values and expectations. Moreover, she felt alienated from almost everyone she knew, and much of her pastoral counseling involved her alienation. Her shame had, as Kaufman suggests, severed many of her "essential human ties."

Shame, Guilt, and the Self

In describing the more relational or interpersonal nature of shame, I have made use of the concept of the self. Simply defined, the self is composed of those personality features, experiences, and activities that are claimed as one's own. Shame and guilt are quickly identified as part of one's own experience and in this respect are not intrinsically different from each other.

> Shame, however, involves more self-consciousness and more self-imaging than guilt. The experience of shame is directly about the *self*, which is the focus of evaluation. In guilt the self is not the central object of negative evaluation, but rather the *thing* done or undone is the focus. In guilt, the self is negatively evaluated in connection with something but is not itself the focus of the experience. Since the self is the focus of awareness in shame, "identity" imagery is also registering as one's own experience, creating a "doubleness" of experience which is characteristic of shame.[28]

One of the functions of shame, then, is protection against the loss of self-boundaries. "Shame functions as a sharp, in fact, painful, reminder that the fantasy experience of the 'other' is vicarious. Shame brings into focal awareness both the self and the 'other,' with the imagery that the 'other' rejects the self. It thus helps to maintain the sense of separate identity by making the self the focus of experience."[29] This view is similar to Helen Merrell Lynd's understanding of how shame can function to spur the search for identity.[30]

Edith Jacobson places the origin of inferiority feelings, which are indeed associated with shame, at an earlier stage in development than does Alexander or Erikson, at the time when the self develops during the first year and a half in life, the so-called narcissistic period. Both shame and inferiority feelings "manifest a person's conflicts with standards that regulate self esteem in terms of pride and superiority rather than moral behavior in relation to others." Shame reactions, according to Jacobson, "range between guilt and inferiority feelings and may be coupled with either of them or both." Shame, inferiority feelings, and feelings of humiliation "develop from deficiencies or failures which betray weakness." They refer to the self with regard "to its power, its intactness, its appearance, and even its moral perfection but not in terms of our loving or hostile impulses and behavior toward others."[31]

Jacobson notes how shame and guilt are often diametrically opposed to each other. "For instance, a person may feel guilty because of his sexual aggression but will be ashamed of impotence." Whereas sadistic impulses are more likely to induce guilt, "passive, dependent leanings, which may cause work inhibitions and hence ineptitude, tend to arouse feelings of shame and inferiority."[32] Although many aspects of this discussion of the self-concept with respect to shame and guilt are useful in understanding Emmie and Tom, perhaps most useful is the realization that in both cases the self—the central features of who they were—became the central issue for pastoral counseling.

Shame and Self-Psychology

The major contributor to recognizing the importance of shame in the development and continuing experience of persons is Heinz Kohut. His influence, at this time, is such that one simply cannot overlook his work. Operating within the psychoanalytic framework, Kohut uses his theoretical understanding of the development of the self in the primary parent-child experience to offer an anthropology that speaks to the entire course of life.[33]

Human beings need the empathic response of others in the first few months of life in order that the self may be adequately structured. They need similar empathy throughout life in order that they may be emotionally nourished. The norm for humankind is not the independent person, but the empathically related one. Kohut's understanding of empathy is the key to his theory. For him empathy is not as much warmth or kindness as it is a disciplined, intuitive understanding of the other. It is the primary method by which we gain knowledge of persons. Early in life the self learns the way in which empathic others experience the world and attempts to adopt this way of knowing other persons through what he or she experiences with them.[34] One of Kohut's major concerns was in keeping his theories what he called "experience-near," in order to be sure that theory was interpreting actual clinical experience rather than having experience conform to theory.

In contrast to the way in which traditional psychoanalytic theory used the term *object* to describe an "other" to whom one is related, Kohut used the term *self-object* to emphasize the self's need for the other. In order to survive and for the self to develop, the individual must internalize or "take in" significant others. When this process does not occur in a satisfactory way, a pathological narcissism results, but the hungry search for the other, the self-object, is not in itself pathological. It is simply expressive of the relational nature of humankind.[35]

Shame develops in Kohut's theory in the process of meeting self-object needs early in a person's life, but also in a way prototypical for later experiences. He identifies two basic types of self-object needs: mirroring and idealizing. The first is associated with the need for recognition and response that is at first grandiose and later, under proper conditions, realisitic. The second is based upon our need to feel a part of a power greater than ourselves which also has a grandiose and later, if things go well, a realistic dimension. When things do not go well in the developmental and continuing relational process, the grandiosity of the self leads to a paralyzing anxiety and self-fragmentation. "Shame arises," says Paul Ornstein, one of Kohut's leading interpreters, "when the self objects do not respond with the expected mirroring, approval, and admiration to the 'boundless exhibitionism' of the grandiose self."[36] In contrast to a view of shame which sees it as the reaction of a relatively weak ego to its failure to live up to the demands of a strong ego ideal within the already constructed self (see Piers and Singer above), Kohut sees shame as occurring in the actual structural formation of the self as well as in self-threatening experiences later in life. In Kohut's theory, shame is a response of the whole self to frustration and rejection rather than a struggle between conflicting parts of the personality. Narcissism, the human phenomenon of the self's overconcern with itself, is the self's attempt to substitute self-care for care by a significant other which is experienced as absent or inadequate.

"If I were asked," says Kohut, "what I consider to be the most important point to be stressed about narcissism I would answer: Its independent line of development, from the primitive to the most mature, adaptive and culturally valuable."[37] Expressing this continuity in a different way, he comments that "experiences during the period of the formation of the self become the prototype of the specific forms of our later vulnerability and security . . . the ups and downs in our self-esteem . . . and of the greater or lesser cohesion of our self during periods of transition."[38] What Kohut affirms is that the narcissistic substitution of self-concern for the shame of reaching out for attention and love and not receiving it is essentially a normal one, i.e., it occurs in everyone, differing only in degree of severity. It is pathological when the rejection is extreme and the compensation for it by the self also has to be extreme. The term *narcissism* then, can be descriptive of the human situation of all of us.

With respect to shame as it appears in this prototypical situation of early life, the self asks for care, and for one reason or another fails to receive it or receive enough of it. The result of not receiving is shame at one's vulnerability and at the strength of one's need for care by the other. The first defense against that shame of exposure is a denial of the need, followed by distancing oneself from the other and a compensatory turning back to the self as a substitute for the rejecting other person. Under optimum circumstances, when the rejection is not severe and consistent, the self may choose to endure the shame and maintain the relationship rather than denying the need and moving away. Under less than optimum circumstances, however, narcissistic grandiosity, which expresses by its action "I don't need anybody," is substituted for the experience of shame.

Kohut's normative term for describing what should happen in early development and what, in effect, is recreated in the therapeutic situation is *optimum frustration*.[39] Self-structure develops in a person as a result of not having his or her needs fully met. He or she is frustrated enough to introject something of the significant other in order to build self-structure. Without frustration or with too much frustration, this would not happen. The situation is optimum when the shame of denial is sufficient to cause the self to create stucture rather than simply to remain a part of the other person, but not so great as to cause the person to retreat from the other and deny his or her relatedness. An interesting illustration may be seen in the situation described to me by a mother of four children. Her youngest child, a two-year-old, came to her asking to be held. The mother was busy with other things and told her that she didn't have time for her then. The daughter's response was a tearful, "My lap's gone."

The situation is instructive at a number of points. The daughter has experienced the closeness of mother's lap and quite naturally claims it as her own. At this point in her development, she has not fully differentiated her self from mother's, but she is aware of her need for care. The mother's denial of her left the daughter vulnerable and open to shame for asking something she did not receive and rage at her not receiving it. Optimally, however, the daughter's feelings will be responded to with empathy by the mother. The daughter's knowing from experience that the lap is not always unavailable allows her to create other ways of finding satisfaction without trying to distance herself from the shame and deny that sometimes she really does need the lap. It will also enable her to create self-structure to substitute for those increasing numbers of times when the mother is unavailable. Discerning the fact that the lap cannot always be hers also helps her to differentiate her self from her mother's. The lap really is her mother's, but because of their special relationship, it is sometimes available for her. The self develops normally when an empathic relationship allows us to experience shame and rage without denying it and distancing ourselves from it.

The psychotherapeutic situation itself creates a comparable situation in which shame naturally reemerges. As Kohut puts it, "Without reference to the specific details of his psychic illness," the "treatment as a whole offends the pride of the analysand, contradicts his fantasy of his independence."[40] Needless to say, this is not only true of psychoanalysis but of almost any helping relationship. I recall one of my counselees, with whom I had been working for some time, expressing her experience of the therapeutic situation something like this: "I feel ashamed that you have seen me—that you know me as well as you do." Later in the same session her words, "I hate depending on you this much," expressed some of the rage and shame that result from the full recognition of human relatedness.

In his focus upon the self, Kohut differed from traditional psychoanalysis in his understanding of the major therapeutic task. Rather than a primary emphasis on the unconscious becoming conscious, his interpretations were more likely to involve a concern with the patient's self. For Kohut it was less important to interpret the meaning of a conflict between the patient's present life and unconscious motivation than to look for and comment upon the injury to the self which the emergence of the formerly unconscious material might represent. When something is revealed through a slip of the tongue, for example, what one most wants to conceal is not the thing that was revealed, but the loss of control in revealing it. "What one is ashamed of is that suddenly something broke through without one's having anything to do with this revelation."

Kohut gives another example of narcissistic injury and the shame to the self involved in the analytic situation with the description of a young man who, as he puts it, "treated me and my attempts at explanations and interpretations at the beginning of the analysis with inimitable condescension. . . . One simply cannot describe it, one has to have heard it to savor fully the expertise with which he tried to destroy my self-confidence, to degrade me." Rather than seeing this as simply negative transference from the past, Kohut understands it as a demonstration of "how he experiences the analysis, how my interpretations are received by *him*—how vulnerable and helpless *he* feels." What is needed as a response to the patient's shame and consequent retaliation is an acknowledgment that the analyst has indeed experienced some pain, but is not overcome by it. Instead he must continue to offer empathy through the expression of his sincere understanding for the position of the patient and how this may be related to similarly shameful-feeling circumstances experienced in the past.[41] The therapeutic experience involves assisting a person to talk about and experience shame within the empathic relationship, gradually expose the grandiose self that was created to push the shame away, and substitute a more realisitic and related self.

What Kohut described and what I have experienced in some of the more intense moments of long-term pastoral counseling is not so much sickness as it is the intensity of human striving to become an adequately structured and functioning self. Although a number of ways in which his work is relevant for a discussion of the problem with human forgiveness are presented in the next two chapters, the most important for us here is Kohut's association of shame with the early, structural formation of the self rather than with some of its later emerging components. Although the degree to which shame is a crippling issue in the life of a person has many variations, Kohut's self-psychology presents shame as a common human problem with which Emmie and Tom and all the rest of us have to deal. Narcissism is not just a diagnostic category applicable to some of us, but a statement of the way things are with all of us to a greater or lesser degree. What Kohut discusses about the treatment of narcissism has relevance for understanding all sorts and conditions of human beings.

Shame and the Essentially Human

As I have already suggested in the discussion of Kohut's work, shame has positive as well as negative functions. Sidney Levin[42] emphasizes this and encourages the development of "shame mastery" as a result of the analytic working-through process. He also notes the value of shame, when not excessive, as a protection against the sexual drive, overexposure to others, and the trauma of rejection. Helen Merrell Lynd presents the positive contribution of shame by insisting that confronting "experiences of shame full in the face" leads to the sense of identity and freedom.[43] She quotes appreciatively a poem of Emily Dickinson:

> Shame need not crouch
> In such an earth as ours;
> Shame, stand erect,
> The universe is yours!

Henry P. Ward discusses shame as a necessity for growth in therapy. To do something differently draws attention to the self. This is a phenomenon common with the experience of shame. Moreover, changing one's defensive pattern usually means that one has not lived up to the expectations of oneself. "In other words," says Ward, "to change requires an encounter with feelings of shame, the effect of which tends to oppose the change. Shame operates then within a negative feedback system and favors the status quo." There is, however, a positive feature in this. It "offers the personality organization the stability essential for certain functions that require time, such as working through, logical reasoning, and so on. Without such stability the ground would be shifting so swiftly that a person might be unable to develop a sense of identity, nor the enduring patterns of behavior crucial to the concept of the self."[44]

Ward distinguishes between voluntary and involuntary

submission to shame. Involuntary shame produces very little growth. To be shamed contributes to one's covering up and increased defensiveness. If, on the other hand, one chooses to experience shame believing in some way that it is necessary for growth, the shame gradually loses its painfulness. One's behavior and experiencing become less inhibited and more free. The analyst deals with shame by demonstrating that it can be survived, by elaborating the costs of avoiding it, by increasing trust in the therapeutic relationship so that the shock of the shame experience appears to be less, and by explicit labeling of the ingredients of the shame experience. Handling the experience with words reduces its power and converts shame into a positive therapeutic force. Ward's summary description of the analysis of shame is less upon ridding the patient of an unpleasant experience than upon "working through" it and integrating it into the total personality.[45]

In concluding this discussion of shame and the problem with human forgiveness by describing some of shame's positive features, I am doing more than acknowledging the social functions of discretion shame, the shame that seeks to avoid shame. Emmie's mother, for example, had imbued her with a great deal of discretion shame. Because of this Elmer's "shamelessness" and lack of discretion were more of a disgrace to her than they would have been to someone without as much social shame. Her shame tolerance was low, and it required a lengthy experience of affirmation in counseling and in other relationships for her to realize that she had not been destroyed by it. Learning to tolerate disgrace shame enabled her to go on with life. She had dealt with her shame by what psychoanalysis has called "working through." What we suffer from in our shame is not a disease to be cured but a dimension of the human condition to be experienced, shared, and used as a dynamic for change.

As I have suggested above and try to demonstrate in more detail later on, when Kohut develops his self-psychology through the discussion of narcissism and the function of shame, he is not just broadening the scope of psychoanalysis but presenting a broad vision of the human. Comparable to what Harry Stack Sullivan suggested about the schizo-phrenic thirty years earlier, the narcissist is important because he or she is so much like all of us and can, therefore, reveal us to ourselves. What Emmie and Tom needed, viewed from my perspective, was to deal with their shame in order to become aware of their guilt or, more specifically, their accountability in and for their lives. Shame is an issue which involves the whole self and its condition. The same is true of human forgiveness. Our forgiveness and the possibility of forgiving those in special relation to us are to be found in the context of the question: "Adam, where art thou?" But we can find forgiving in ourselves only when we discover our relationship to one who calls us out of our hiding places.

As in the first chapter, however, we are left here with further questions. How do we accept our shame and discover our guilt? How do pastors assist their parishioners in doing this? And how is this different from the way in which human forgiveness has most often been addressed? Again, I leave these questions until later and move on to consider the primary defenses that persons use to defend themselves against experiencing their shame—power and righteousness.

Notes

1. *Funk and Wagnalls Standard Dictionary*, International Ed. (New York: Funk and Wagnalls, 1970), p. 1155.
2. Carl Schneider, *Shame, Exposure and Privacy* (Boston: Beacon Press, 1977), p. 20.
3. Ibid., p. 22.
4. Ibid., pp. 25, 28.
5. An early recognition of the importance of shame in pastoral care appeared in James N. Lapsley's "A Psycho-Theological Appraisal of the New Left," *Theology Today* 25, no. 4 (January 1969): 446-61. A more recent recognition of shame's importance appears in the fourth chapter of Donald Capps's book, *Life Cycle Theory and Pastoral Care* (Philadelphia: Fortress Press, 1983).
6. S. J. De Vries, "Shame," *Interpreter's Dictionary of the Bible* R–Z (Nashville: Abingdon Press, 1962): 305-6, and J. P. Thornton-Deusbery, "Shame," *A Theological Wordbook of the Bible*, ed. Alan Richardson (London: SCM Press Ltd., 1950), p. 225.
7. De Vries, "Shame," p. 306.

8. Johannes Pedersen, *Israel: Its Life and Culture* 1-2 (London: Oxford University Press, 1926), pp. 239-44.

9. Lyn Bechtel Huber, "The Biblical Experience of Shame/Shaming: The Social Experience of Shame/Shaming in Biblical Israel in Relation to Its Use as Religious Metaphor" (Ann Arbor: University Microfilms, 1983), pp. 203-4. She notes that this is also the conclusion of Krister Stendahl in his essay, "The Apostle Paul and the Introspective Conscience of the West," in *Paul Among the Jews and Gentiles* (Philadelphia: Fortress Press, 1976).

10. Huber, "Biblical Experience of Shame," pp. 207-8.

11. Dietrich Bonhoeffer, *Ethics* (London: SCM Press, 1955), p. 145.

12. Ibid., pp. 145-48.

13. Claus Westermann, *Genesis 1–11* (Minneapolis: Augsburg Publishing House, 1984), pp. 250-51.

14. Gerhard von Rad, *Genesis: A Commentary* (Philadelphia: The Westminster Press, 1961), pp. 88-89.

15. Franz Alexander, *The Scope of Psychoanalysis* (New York: Basic Books, 1961), pp. 131-33.

16. Ibid., p. 135.

17. Eric H. Erikson, *Childhood and Society* (New York: W. W. Norton, 1950), pp. 252-53.

18. Silvan S. Tomkins, *Affect, Imagery, Consciousness, Vol. 2: The Negative Affects* (New York: Springer, 1963), p. 118.

19. Helen B. Lewis, *Shame and Guilt in Neurosis* (New York: International Universities Press, 1971), pp. 33-36.

20. Ibid., p. 36.

21. Gerhart Piers and Milton B. Singer, *Shame and Guilt: A Psychoanalytic and a Cultural Study* (New York: W. W. Norton, 1971. Copyright 1953 by Charles C. Thomas), pp. 23-24.

22. Ibid., pp. 25-26.

23. Lewis, *Shame and Guilt*, p. 27.

24. Gershen Kaufman, *Shame: The Power of Caring* (Cambridge, Mass.: Shenkman Publishing Company, 1980), p. 15.

25. Ibid., pp. 42-43.

26. Ibid., p. 76.

27. Ibid., p. 33.

28. Lewis, *Shame and Guilt*, pp. 30-31.

29. Ibid., p. 25.

30. Helen Merrell Lynd, *On Shame and the Search for Identity* (New York: Science Editions, 1961), p. 21.

31. Edith Jacobson, *The Self and the Object World* (New York: International Universities Press, 1964), p. 145-46.

32. Ibid., p. 147.

33. One of the extended critiques of Kohut's view of shame is that of Leon Wurmser, *The Masks of Shame* (Baltimore: Johns Hopkins University Press, 1981), who says that his book is "riveted to the premise of conflict." "I have written," says Wurmser, "in the conviction that only a conflict psychology, one based in the study of clashing forces or contradictory parts of the personality, can do justice to the great frequency and variety of shame affects and shame conflicts" (p. 15). Kohut's work is based on a different premise, and I find Kohut more statisfying and convincing.

34. Heinz Kohut, *The Nature of Psychoanalytic Cure* (Chicago: The University of Chicago Press, 1984), pp. 52-53, 63.

35. Heinz Kohut, *The Analysis of the Self* (New York: International Universities Press, 1971), pp. 300-307.

36. Paul H. Ornstein, "Introduction," *The Search for the Self: Selected Writings of Heinz Kohut: 1950–1978,* ed. and with an introduction by Paul H. Ornstein, 2 vols. (New York: International Universities Press, 1978), 1:69.

37. Heinz Kohut, "Narcissism and Narcissistic Rage," *The Psychoanalytic Study of the Child* 27 (New York: Quadrangle, 1972): 362.

38. Ibid., pp. 368-69.

39. Kohut, *Analysis of the Self,* p. 50. Cf. also "Narcissism as a Resistance and as a Driving Force in Psychoanalysis," *The Search for the Self* 2:555.

40. Kohut, "Narcissism as Resistance and as a Driving Force," p. 549.

41. Ibid., pp. 551-52.

42. Sidney Levin, "Some Metapsychological Considerations on the Differentiation Between Shame and Guilt," *International Journal of Psychoanalysis* 48 (1967): 267-76.

43. Lynd, *On Shame and the Search for Identity,* pp. 209-10.

44. Henry P. Ward, "Shame—A Necessity for Growth in Therapy," *American Journal of Psychotherapy* 26 (1972): 236.

45. Ibid., p. 242.

Defending Against Shame with Rage and Power

F orgive us our sins—*as we surrender our power to forgive the sins of others.*

It is seldom possible to deal with shame without first responding to the ways in which a person defends against experiencing it. Gershen Kaufman, in his study of shame, identifies five such defenses: rage, contempt, striving for power, perfectionism, and transfer of blame.[1] As I have observed it, contempt has not appeared as a distinct strategy of defense. On the one hand, it is a variation of rage; on the other hand, an expression of power or moral superiority over another. Blaming can certainly be a defense against shame, but it is often experienced in a much more general way—as an avoidance of the honest communication of whatever one feels. A person blames to objectify and express whatever is hurting in terms of the behavior of someone else and to avoid the anxiety of having to experience and communicate that hurt. Blame can also be a way in which a person attempts to demonstrate being in the right.[2] Shame, therefore, is only one of the experiences avoided by blame. Finally, rather than viewing perfectionism as a defense in its own right, I prefer to deal with it as a dimension of being right or righteous.

Obviously, rage, power, and righteousness are psychological phenomena that need to be examined psychologically.

They are also phenomena that have often been interpreted ethically and theologically in the light of Christian faith and practice. I have no doubt that I have "seen" them so often in clinical experience because of my own involvement in and commitment to that faith. I believe, furthermore, that an adequate psychological understanding of them can assist in the process of Christian interpretation. In my view, part of the problem with human forgiveness has been an inadequate psychological understanding of these three phenomena and the way they affect relationships with those who are most important to us.

Franz Alexander, in a paper discussed in the previous chapter, described shame and rage as the "two principal experiential and behavioral manifestations of disturbed narcissistic equilibrium." Most of the persons with whom I have shared the struggle with forgiving have, in my opinion, been dealing with that kind of disturbance—an offense, a brokenness in relationship which questioned the whole structure of their selfhood. Emmie's rejection by her husband, for example, seemed to reactivate an early experience of rejection by her mother, so that her self-structure was shaken. Pastoral counseling was a slow, tedious process of assisting in the restructuring of her self, not just dealing with her "problems."

Heinz Kohut's self-psychology is a major resource in understanding this process. In Kohut's view persons respond to actual or anticipated injury to the self with "shamefaced withdrawal (flight) or with narcissistic rage (fight)."[3] If we apply Kohut's theory to injuries like those experienced by Emmie and Tom—marital infidelity and abandonment by a parent—what happens is that, on the one hand, the injured person may flee from the problem, denying it or denying the extent of the injury, thus avoiding to some degree the experience of shame. Or, on the other hand, he or she may choose a way to fight, through the use of power or the affirmation of righteousness.

Religion has had a great deal to say about both of these defenses and has, for the most part, not viewed them as defenses. It has, for example, often encouraged denial and

[66]

distancing oneself from the problem and the anger associated with it, suggesting that the goal of forgiving is most likely to be achieved in that way. Religion has also been involved in a person's use of power. An eye for an eye, turning the other cheek, having the power to forgive have all been responses to human hurt involving the use of the self's power. Being in the right or righteousness has also been a response advocated by religion. The person who has been hurt may have been encouraged by a pastor or Christian friend to examine the situation to see whether or not "it was his fault," and being able to determine that it was not has been widely understood as helpful in easing, if not eliminating, the pain.

My concern is not so much to point out the inadequacies of these responses to self-injury as to suggest that this kind of hurt is so threatening that it naturally involves whatever religion one has and whatever one's religion seems to advocate as relief. Religious response to self-injury can be more appropriate, however, if the most commonly used defenses against shame can be understood in a more nearly adequate way. In order to move toward this kind of understanding, I first examine the state of rage as it is understood psychologically and, more specifically, Kohut's view of narcissistic rage as a "prototype of human aggression." I move then to addressing the ways in which this rage is used defensively to avoid the experience of shame—through the use of power and powerlessness. In the next chapter, I examine self-righteous rage and the defensive use of "being right." I discuss *rage* rather than anger not just because Kohut and other psychological theorists use that term. In recent years, the term *anger* has become somewhat domesticated. Rage, in contrast, reflects more adequately humankind's primitive and irrational response to self-injury which most of us would like to forget—at least in ourselves.

Rage as a Defense of the Self

Kohut's view of narcissistic rage is an argument against the theory of aggression which suggests that "a tendency to kill is deeply rooted in man's psychobiological makeup and stems from his animal past." This theory, he says, is a "comforting illusion that human pugnacity could be easily abolished if only our material needs were satisfied" and contributes "little to the understanding of aggression as a psychological phenomenon." Instead we should focus "our attention on human aggression as it arises from the matrix of archaic narcissism, i.e., on the phenomenon of narcissistic rage."

The term *narcissistic rage* refers to only one specific band in a wide spectrum of experiences of rage, but these experiences exist on a continuum with one another and have a "common metapsychological substance." Wherever that rage experience exists on the continuum of intensity, it can be recognized as narcissistic or self-threatening by "the need for revenge, for righting a wrong, for undoing a hurt by whatever means, and a deeply anchored, unrelenting compulsion in the pursuit of all these aims." Kohut speaks of the "shame-prone," "narcissistically vulnerable" individual. By this he means a person who has had powerful experiences of shame during the narcissistic or self-formative period of life. Such persons, he says, respond to a potentially shame-provoking situation by inflicting or imagining they are inflicting on others those narcissistic injuries which they are most afraid of suffering themselves. The shame-prone individual "does not recognize his opponent as a center of independent initiative with whom he happens to be at cross-purposes." The opponent is, rather, "*a flaw in a narcissitically perceived reality. He is a recalcitrant part of an expanded self over which the shame-prone individual expects to exercise full control and whose mere independence or other-ness is an offense.*"[4]

The target of our mature aggressions, in contrast, is experienced as separate from ourselves. Kohut acknowledges that everyone reacts to shame-provoking injuries with embarrassment and anger, but those who "are in the grip of narcissistic rage show total lack of empathy toward the offender." This explains, he says, the unmodifiable wish to blot out the offense which was perpetrated against the grandiose self and the unforgiving fury which arises. . . . The emphatic observer will understand the deeper significance of the often seemingly minor irritant which has provoked an attack of narcissistic rage and will not be taken aback by the seemingly disproportionate severity of the reaction.[5]

The transformation of narcissistic rage—and this is important in our attempt to understand the problem with human forgiveness—"is not achieved directly—e.g., via appeals to the ego to increase its control over the angry impulses—but is brought about indirectly, secondary to the gradual transformation of the matrix of narcissism from which the rage arose." Change takes place, in other words, not by directly attacking the defense, but by relating empathically to the defending person. When this strengthening of the self occurs, a person can develop realistic rather than grandiose ambitions and "maturely modulated aggressions will be employed in the service of a securely established self and in the service of cherished values."[6]

Such transformation is made possible, according to Kohut, by the analyst's "nonhypocritical attitude toward narcissism." As I have stated earlier, narcissism as Kohut understands it is not primarily a pathology which the analyst is attempting to cure but a psychological phenomenon which has its own line of development and which, as Kohut puts it, "neither should—nor indeed could—be relinquished." It is the empathic attitude toward this human phenomenon which can reduce resistance and facilitate the analytic process. It is a slow process because the analyst cannot immediately align himself or herself with the patient's reality ego but must be tolerant of the rage which may emerge when the patient's narcissistic needs are not immediately and totally fulfilled.

Our therapeutic aim with regard to narcissistic rage is neither the direct transformation of the rage into constructive aggression nor the direct establishment of controls over the rage by the autonomous ego. Our principal goal is the gradual transformation of the narcissistic matrix from which the rage arises. If this objective is reached, then the aggressions in the narcissistic sector of the personality will be employed in the service of the realistic ambitions and purposes of a securely established self.[7]

What this means may be seen most clearly in presenting two of Kohut's clinical examples. The first case involved a man who was inordinately dependent on idealized persons whose praise he craved. He did not have an adequate supply of what Kohut calls "narcissistic sustenance," or affirmation and confirmation early in life of who he was by significant others. Because of this deficiency of the self, when these contemporary idealized persons were unresponsive to him, he became enraged and criticized them with bitterness and sarcasm. By extensive working through of the relationship with the analyst—experiencing and understanding how he idealized significant others and receiving additional affirmation of his self through the analyst's empathy—what Kohut refers to as the "structural defect" in his self became ameliorated and his rage changed. His criticism of others became more realistic and tinged with humor. Moreover, he increasingly sought the companionship of peers—those whom he saw as in a similar situation to himself—rather than seeking recognition from authorities.

Another of Kohut's cases describes a man who often severely punished his eight-year-old son. In the course of analysis, he became aware that when he felt frustrated by persons who could nourish his deprived self, he reacted with violent anger. He could at first not relate this to his behavior toward his son and attempted to justify his actions by claiming that "consistency and unbending justice were better for his son than ill-placed kindness and unprincipled tolerance." What Kohut calls his "moralistic punitiveness" began to subside after the memory that his mother had "always reacted with severe, morally buttressed punishments" when he had attempted to extricate himself from her complete control. His rage toward his son appeared to occur when the son's "misbehavior" seemed to reflect increased independence from the father. His empathy with his son "increased as the patient began to master his narcissistic involvement with alter-ego figures and grasped the fact that he was repeating a crucial situation from his own childhood."[8]

What the analyst has done in these cases has been to offer empathy, patient understanding, and a significant relationship within which the defective relationships from the past could be examined and through which additional emotional nourishment could be offered. The injury and the rage have not been directly addressed but have been dealt with in the context of an empathic response to the impoverished self. An accurate understanding of empathy is most important here. It may involve warmth and kindness but is not primarily that. Rather, empathy, as Kohut presents it, is that disciplined, intuitive understanding that offers in its expression a model of a caring human being, useful information about oneself, and genuine experience in relationship which is the real turf on which life is lived. This is not the way that Kohut would say it, but it seems to me to be an accurate expression of his point of view.

Empathy as Kohut describes it may be understood as offering a "corrective emotional experience." In contrast to psychoanalytic orthodoxy, Kohut insists that he believes both in the curative effect of such experience and its place in psychoanalytic practice.[9] The designation "corrective emotional experience" is, however, far too narrow to describe what Kohut means by empathy. The experience is more than emotional, and it may be understood as more normative than corrective. Experience in such a relationship does indeed satisfy some of our emotional hunger, but the term *corrective* suggests that it is designed to correct a particular past error in management, and this is not the case.

An empathic relationship provides useful experience in addressing life. It strengthens the person by eventually providing a more functional self, not by attempting to erase his or her problems. I believe with Kohut that narcissistic rage can usefully be understood as a "prototype of human aggression," and that sensitivity to self-injury and shame is essential for the pastoral counselor. As I have claimed in the previous chapter, Kohut's self theory is not simply an approach to a particular kind of pathology in theory and clinical practice. It is, rather, a broadly based anthropology which makes significant affirmations about what is normatively human and how that is expressed relationally.

With respect to the problem with human forgiveness, Kohut's understanding of narcissistic rage is a strong reminder that behavioral attempts to deal with anger are not adequate to confront life as it is or people as they are. Persons who have suffered self-injury do not "get over" their anger by either suppressing or expressing it. Their perception of reality is so influenced by what has happened to them that their rage cannot be dealt with apart from the way in which they are experiencing themselves. The person who has injured them is, as Kohut puts it, "a flaw in a narcissistically perceived reality," so that discussing what should be done in relation to that person—forgiveness or anything else—is seldom worth the trouble. The prior task is relationally binding the wounds without concern for what should be done to get life back in order again.

Unfortunately, religion's response has too often been to try to fix things, expecting lasting results, for example, from simply announcing God's forgiveness. If we are forgiven, then we should be forgiving. This may be true—and in many ways I believe it is—but human beings have significant capacities for avoiding that truth. They simply are not what they ought to be, nor do they do what they should in spite of impressive religious announcements and expectations. Undoubtedly the announcement of forgiveness is important, but the schedule upon which that announcement is apprehended by the forgiven one remains highly unpredictable. Kohut's view of narcissistic rage is another reminder for us to take human recalcitrance seriously. Neither patients nor parishioners do what they ought to do. And after all these years as a pastoral counselor, I still have difficulty living with that fact.

Moreover, with respect to rage, religion has often complicated rather than facilitated our dealing with it. Twenty-odd years ago when I went as chaplain to a university hospital, ministers were not allowed to visit in the psychiatric unit because they were thought to get in the way of the patient's recovery. My first efforts in that area, therefore, were in getting to know the staff and letting them get to know me. After several months I was called to visit a patient and requested by the staff to tell him that the Bible didn't mean what the patient thought it did. I said that I was not sure I could do that, but that I would see the patient and try to find out what the problem was.

Not surprisingly, when I got to the patient's room I found that he was reading the Sermon on the Mount and was quite agitated by what Jesus had to say about anger. The staff of the psychiatric unit wanted a minister to tell the patient that it was all right to express anger and that thinking about it and doing it were not the same thing. I had no trouble with most of that request. It can be all right to express anger—not always, of course—but certainly when getting over one's illness involves identifying and expressing one's feelings in a safe place to do just that. The other part of the request, however, was more complicated. Thinking and doing it are not the same thing, and the Sermon on the Mount does not really say that they are. What it does seem to say, however, is that we are responsible for our "hearts" as well as our behavior and that simply doing or not doing something is not the main issue in life. That issue can seldom be dealt with in one pastoral call. Fortunately, the staff in the psychiatric unit found that it was useful to have a minister around to do more than interpret problem verses in the Bible.

Part of the problem with human forgiveness has been religion's attempt to deal with the rage evoked by injury to the self rather than recognizing that it is the *heart* or self *with the rage in it* that is the problem. The implication of this for pastoral counseling and for ministry in general is that we assist persons in dealing with their rage not by encouraging them either to express or suppress it. Rather, the degree of its intensity is an indicator of the degree of injury to the self, and self-injury requires the offering of empathy longer than our impatience and desire for visible results would like to allow. I examine rage in the next chapter from a somewhat different perspective but with similar conclusions. At this point, however, I move from the discussion of how rage can be a part of the problem with human forgiveness to the complications presented by power and powerlessness as a defense against shame.

Defending the Self with Power or Powerlessness

In pastoral counseling with Tom, the central issue was his becoming more realistic about himself, his personal power and strength, and feeling more comfortable using that power in relationships. The problems which he presented were related to his experience of feeling abandoned by his father in early adolescence and whatever defective parenting may have occurred before that. His primary defense against the shame he felt was using his power or powerlessness. Prior to the interview which I presented in the first chapter and to which I return now, Tom's father, in a long-distance telephone conversation, had shared some of his feelings of weakness and hopelessness prior to divorcing Tom's mother. As he reported this to me, Tom described a lump in his throat which he felt then and felt now in talking to me.

Pastor: What's the lump? Discovering that he had problems too?
Tom: Wondering if I really can forgive him.
Pastor: It's hard to give up that power.
Tom: Power?
Pastor: You sound more like a priest than a son. Go back to the lump in your throat.

In the telephone conversation Tom's father had apparently revealed more of his humanness and vulnerability than Tom was ready to accept, so Tom clung to his old defense, power—in this case, the power to forgive.

It is striking how what may be the most common expression of Christian faith—the Lord's Prayer—may suggest to a person who is struggling with his or her inadequacy and shame the possibility of using power as a defense. Further exposition of the meaning of the petition "forgive us our debts as we forgive our debtors" can be deferred until later, but one can see how that phrase might be seen as a gift of power. In the midst of one's feeling of powerlessness to deal with shame-causing injury, the prayer can remind us of the power to forgive or to withhold forgiveness. In twenty years of pastoral counseling, I have heard Tom's "I don't know whether or not I can forgive" again and again and only recently have been able to call it what I think it is, a self-protective use of power. Before continuing with this discussion of the power to forgive, however, it seems important to discuss power psychologically in order to understand more clearly the way it can be used defensively.

Psychological Interpretation of Power and Powerlessness

The striving for power is, perhaps, most frequently a direct attempt to compensate for the sense of inferiority in relation to another and the shame that it produces. To the extent one is successful in gaining power over others, one becomes increasingly less vulnerable to futher shame. Power can also be used to compensate for shame which was internalized earlier in life. According to Gershen Kaufman,

> To the degree that one can now feel powerful in relation to others, through gaining power over them, one has reversed roles from the way it was in early life. . . . The power strategy may or may not include longings for vengeance and the active seeking of revenge. But it does encompass instances in which security is to be won through control and self-esteem is to be amassed through power.[10]

In this section I discuss three psychological perspectives on power and powerlessness. W. W. Meissner's psychoanalytic view; an existential interpretation from Rollo May; and a family systems perspective from Jay Haley.

W. W. Meissner, in his extensive study of the paranoid process, presents a useful interpretation of how power and powerlessness can both function defensively. He uses the case of Mr. James J. as an illustration of how the paranoid process operates in relatively healthy persons. In a general statement about paranoia, he notes that the paranoid does not recognize

> that he has more power to influence his environment than he thinks he does. He has little sense of his effects on others. This is quite apparent clinically in paranoid patients who see themselves as victims without any sense of what they have done to elicit or provoke action against themselves.[11]

Meissner describes his patient Jimmy as viewing every relationship, every context in which he had to deal with other people "as a field in which the forces of power and submission played themselves out." If he were not in possession of absolute power, he felt in danger of complete subjugation and vulnerability. On the one hand, "he recalled as a child that he always felt that he was helpless and submitted to his parents' power, particularly that of his mother." But, on the other hand, when his parents gave in to his wishes, "he felt a frightening sense of power over them and felt that he was bad and demanding to make them do something against their wills."

During most of his analysis, however, Jimmy emphasized the side that saw others as powerful and himself as powerless. In the analysis itself, he viewed the analyst as the powerful one and himself the helpless victim. "He could not run the risk of striving to gain what he wanted by active assertion, so he adopted the position of the passive and dependent child. The weak and defective baby was not a threat to anyone, but he got his way by being helpless and weak."[12]

The kind of special relations that are a part of family life present an inescapable situation of power in the relationship of one family member to another. Meissner's patient Jimmy may be seen as an example of this in his use of helplessness to control others. Either power or powerlessness may be used to establish position or control. The dependency of family member upon family member presents a vulnerability which is often defended against with power tactics. This can be seen most clearly in the literature of family therapy, both in the relationships within the family and the relationship of the family therapist to the family. Although those who write about family systems are more likely to view the preservation of homeostasis within the family system as the major reason for the use of power, what they say about power and powerlessness within the family can be seen from the perspective of the family member using it as an attempt to compensate for a sense of inferiority in relation to another and its consequent shame.

Rollo May identifies five kinds of power: exploitative, manipulative, competitive, nutrient, and integrative. The first three are those which are often used—and this is my interpretation, not May's—to defend against shame. Exploitative power "is exercised by those who have been radically rejected. . . . Exploitative power always presupposes violence or the threat of violence. In this kind of power there is, strictly speaking, no choice or spontaneity at all on the part of the victims." Manipulative power is power *over* another person. It is the power to persuade, outwit, or induce behavior by means of guilt or implied obligation. Here too there is very little spontaneity and freedom of choice left to the person defending with it or to the person defending against it. Competitive power is power *against* another. "In its negative form, it consists of one person going up not because of anything he does or any merit he has, but because his opponent goes down."[13] In a later book, May comments on how the term *control* is often used as a substitute term for power. Control "puts the accent on *my* right to exert power over *you*. It would be clearer to use the word *power* to begin with."[14]

Because May contrasts the negative or defensive uses of power with the positive values of spontaneity and choice, part of the treatment of his patient Mercedes, whom he describes as "an individual with practically no sense of her own power or spontaneity or choice," involved using his own power as her therapist to require her to decide when and if she wanted to come to psychotherapy. He scheduled no regular appointments but used his own manipulative power to demonstrate the power she had to decide about

[77]

her life, beginning with whether or not she wanted to make use of him. Having used variations of this technique myself, I can see the value of it. It is clearly manipulative and, as such, needs to be constantly subject to the criticism of whether the end of actualizing a person's decision-making and consequent power over his or her life justifies the means. Manipulation can quickly become mechanical and impersonal and, as such, inconsistent with a pastoral relationship. Nevertheless, demonstrations of a person's use of power can often be far more effective than oral interpretation.

The psychotherapist who is probably most identified with the therapeutic use of power is family systems theorist and therapist Jay Haley. He describes relationships in the family as significantly determined by people struggling to achieve control over one another, and the therapeutic relationship as one in which patients engage in similar power struggles with the therapist. "Therapists, therefore according to Haley, need to outwit and manipulate patients in such a way as to defeat their resistance and subtle uncooperativeness. . . . Since symptoms are seen as ways of dealing with people, therapy must provide other ways of dealing with people."[15] The important thing about a symptom—and this could be any behavior that affects the family system—"is the advantage it gives the patient in gaining control of what is to happen in a relationship with someone else."[16]

My purpose here is not to make an extensive presentation of Haley's views or to suggest that they describe what ought to happen in family therapy. There is, however, an interesting parallel between the way an individual defends himself or herself against shame and the way in which a family defends itself against change. The typical situation that calls for family therapy is one in which one family member, usually one of the children, has an unacceptable behavioral problem. One of the parents asks a therapist to help get rid of the unacceptable behavior. The family therapist assumes that the troublesome symptom is functioning in some way to maintain the family balance and defend it against change and that the "problem" is more the way the system functions than it is the symptom itself.

The therapist attempts to deal with the whole family—more often than not by seeing them together—attempting to change what is happening in the family rather than addressing the symptom. In doing so the therapist exposes the family to "public" view. The therapist sees and discusses openly the "secret" way in which the family operates. Thus the family defends against its shame at being seen through efforts to control the therapist that are similar to the ways in which family members use their power to control one another. In their emphasis on the system, family therapists do not usually talk about shame because it is an affective experience of the individual. The family therapist's exposing the family's way of operating to question and comment, however, creates a shame dynamic not unlike that of an individual medical patient who undresses to be examined by a physician. The troubled family is exposed, and it defends its personal relationships and structure against the therapist's proposed change by using the kind of power it is most accustomed to using.

Haley understands symptoms as manipulative ploys which operate outside the awareness of the patient. The family member with the disturbing symptom sees it as something that has happened to him or her. The wife who compulsively washes her hands says that she has "a hand-washing compulsion" rather than "I compulsively wash my hands." If she acknowledges that she can control her behavior, then she loses the power of the symptom to defend herself against a husband in relation to whom she feels powerless. The therapist's task is to get the patient to discover in some way that he or she lives in a relational rather than a circumstantial world.

Although his theories and methods have changed over the last twenty or so years, one of Haley's abiding concerns has been the interpersonal use of power. In a family interview he begins jockeying for position right away.

As the family enters, he studies their interactions to learn how power is distributed in the system. He notes who is dominant and who is submissive, who is aggressive and who is defensive. He also pays careful attention to how family members relate to him. . . . As the family members talk with each other, Haley observes how the family is organized. Who sides with whom? Who has the most power, and who has the least?[17]

The therapeutic effort also involves the use of power. The details of how power is used therapeutically are not important for us here. What happens, however, when therapy is effective is that the family is taught that power can be used in a way that benefits all members of the system. Family members discover that relationships are more important than circumstances and that persons in relation to their significant others have enough power to change things so that they do not need to use their power to defend themselves. The family becomes comfortable enough with the shame of being exposed by the therapist to use the power previously used for defending the status quo to change what needs to be changed.

There are those in the family therapy field who argue against the power motif as a major interpretive mode for what happens in the therapeutic process.[18] My discussion of power in the family is not intended to take a position on that issue other than to say that theorists like Haley have expanded our ability to recognize and use interpersonal power.[19] What appears to be powerlessness can often be seen to be a position of power in the sense of its effect upon others within the family.

A familiar situation to anyone who works with families professionally or observes them carefully is one in which the son who has completed his education is still living at home and depending upon his parents for continuation of the old pattern of family relationship. A middle-aged physician and his wife consulted me along with their twenty-three-year-old son and younger daughter. The son, they said, was creating havoc with their lives because of his irresponsibility. He was staying out late, making noise that disturbed the father when he did come in, and not getting up in the morning in time to get to his job. His mother tried everything she could think of to get him out of bed so that he would not lose his job. The son expressed his unhappiness because his parents, particularly his mother, kept meddling in his life.

The reader can quickly perceive what *ought* to happen. The son ought to become more responsible and the parents less meddling, but like most of us, in spite of the fact that they were a *good* family, they did not do as they *ought* to do. Each was too busy preserving the family system from change, and in spite of the discomfort of living in a situation which they have outgrown, each family member gained something by the son's not "growing up." The mother, who had felt abandoned over the years by her physician husband, maintained her closeness to the other male in the family and through him disturbed her husband's sleep at night. The father maintained his position of power by continuing to stay out of the family as much as possible and getting his wife to take responsibility for things and, of course, the blame when things don't go well. The daughter maintained her position as the "good" child.

Although I have not discussed all of the combinations of relationships within the family, it is clear that each family member has significant power to control the others and maintain the system as it has been. Moreover, in relation to me as one to whom they had come for help, they found ways to defend themselves against the shame of being seen and seeing things as they appeared to an outsider. Finding an alternative pattern of living that was more satisfying involved deciding whether or not they really wanted some change, discovering other ways to look at the family situation, and taking enough action to begin to change the homeostatic balance of things. Involved in all of that is getting more comfortable with the shame of being seen by the therapist and in a different way by other members of the family.

Tom's Power to Forgive

Specifically examining the power to forgive as a defense against shame, my counselee Tom wonders if he can ever forgive his father. What better way to hold on to an old and familiar relationship than to maintain an incomplete transaction, a debit on what Ivan Nagy has called the "ledger of justice"? As long as Tom withholds his forgiveness, his father still owes him something, and the relationship is maintained. If the forgiveness is offered and the debit removed, relationship to the father may be lost. To be sure, Tom is not conscious of the process I am describing—of the power "advantage" he holds in not forgiving. He is, however, in a comparable position to the son in the physician's family—holding on to the past because the past, though uncomfortable, is familiar. Though his fear of change is an irrational one, Tom acts as if a new relationship with his father might reveal more of his inadequacy as a man.

In addition to the "advantage" that withholding forgiveness offers by preserving the past, it gives Tom something which his father does not appear to have—forgiveness understood almost like a possession. It is like a trump card that can be played at any time to show who is really in charge. Uncertain about his personal power because, among other things, of his inability to substitute for his mother's absent husband, Tom can always have his power to forgive available. Should he offer it, however, his advantage would be lost, and his strength in relation to his father would have to be evaluated on other grounds. Moreover, his father would no longer need him for forgiveness, and perhaps, he fears—again irrationally—the relationship would be broken. There are clear advantages to Tom in not forgiving—advantages that may be thought of in terms of power to defend oneself against the shame of inadequacy and inferiority.

Another striking element in this use of power may be seen in Tom's ways of describing his situation, and this is the way that I have usually heard it described by others. He wonders whether or not he can forgive his father. In putting it this way, Tom is saying, "It appears to be beyond my control to do what you, my religious tradition, and others are implying that I should do." Thus, Tom is holding on to power as a circumstance which has been created for him, perhaps to make up for the shame he has endured, rather than assuming that he can do what he wants to in the relationship. In effect, he feels powerless to give up his power. Adapting the old cliché to Tom's situation, "This is something bigger than both of us, and I can't help using it."

Theological Interpretation of Power and Powerlessness

Moving this far into a discussion of personal power pushes one of my persuasion and experience from psychological to theological interpretation. To reflect on the use and misuse of power is, for me, to think of Reinhold Niebuhr. To wonder why Tom and others might hold on to the power to forgive as a way of protecting themselves from shame calls to mind Niebuhr's understanding of the origin of sin—that it is neither an inevitable consequence of the human situation nor an act of sheer and perverse individual defiance of God. Niebuhr's statement of the "given" of the human condition still seems almost unmatched in my experience for its psychological usefulness. Using Kierkegaard as his major authority, he argues that humankind's response to anxiety is the major contributor to sin. "Anxiety is the inevitable concomitant of the paradox of freedom and finiteness in which man is involved." Anxiety itself, however, is not sin.

> It must be distinguished from sin partly because it is its precondition and not its actuality, and partly because it is the basis of all human creativity as well as the precondition of sin. Man is anxious not only because his life is limited and dependent and yet not so limited that he does not know of his limitations. He is also anxious because he does not know the limits of his possibilities. He can do nothing and regard it perfectly done, because higher possibilities are revealed in each achievement. All human actions stand under seemingly limitless possibilities.[20]

This statement of the human condition will be useful later in interpreting the defense of righteousness as well as the defense of power. Continuing with Niebuhr's analysis:

It resides in the inclination of man, either to deny the contingent character of his existence (in pride and self-love) or to escape from his freedom (in sensuality). Sensuality represents an effort to escape from the freedom and the infinite possibilities of spirit by becoming lost in the detailed processes, activities and interests of existence, an effort which results inevitably in unlimited devotion to limited values. . . . Biblical and Christian thought has maintained with a fair degree of consistency that pride is more basic than sensuality and that the latter is, in some way, derived from the former.[21]

Niebuhr argues against the psychological explanation that suggests that human insecurity is a result of the pressures of competitive civilization or other societal pressures. "The ego," he says, "does not feel secure and therefore grasps for more power in order to make itself secure. It does not regard itself as sufficiently significant or respected or feared and therefore seeks to enhance its position in nature and in society. . . . The truth is," he says, "that man is tempted by the basic insecurity of human existence to make himself doubly secure and by the insignificance of his place in the total scheme of life to prove his significance."[22]

Although I am not convinced that sensuality is, as Niebuhr suggests, derived from pride or that it is the best term for the human choice to be less than one is, his work argues strongly for the view that either power or powerlessness can be used to defend oneself against shame and anxiety. Jürgen Moltmann, in his *Theology of Hope,* has questioned the primacy of pride in human sin. If, as he suggests, faith depends on hope for its life, "then the sin of unbelief is manifestly grounded in hopelessness," and temptation "consists not so much in the titanic desire to be as God, but in weakness, timidity, weariness, not wanting to be what God requires of us."[23]

Harvey Cox, arguing for "a doctrine of sin that will not encourage deference and dependency," has suggested "that the venerable old term sloth describes our spiritual debility better than the word pride does. Sloth means being *less* than instead of *more* than man."[24] Brian Grant, a pastoral theologian, has discussed sloth from the practical point of view of one who encounters the traditional seven deadly sins in the persons he sees in pastoral counseling. He understands the origin of sloth to be in learning as children that "our efforts would not affect the world" and in having parents discourage every independent act. The sin continues in adulthood when a person maintains the childhood pattern of living as if the control of life were completely external to himself or herself. As Grant puts it, addressing himself directly to the person struggling with this sin, "What you have failed to notice as you grew older is that the circumstances which once made you powerless have in fact changed. Now the power to act lies within you. . . . it is utterly crucial that you discover your own power to act."[25]

Cox interprets the same human phenomenon that Grant describes in the persons he sees in counseling as it appears in relation to the larger issues of life and society, when it "takes the form of hiding behind a speciality, a lack of knowledge, a fear of involvement, which become rationalizations for not assuming one's share in the responsible use of power in the world." This, he describes, using the Genesis story, as "leaving it to the snake."

> Eve shared with Adam the assignment of exercising mastery over all the creatures of the field. Her "original" misdeed was not eating the forbidden fruit at all. Before she reached for the fruit she had already surrendered her position of power and responsibility over one of the animals, the serpent, and let it tell her what to do. Thus self-doubt, hesitant anxiety, and dependency actually preceded that fatal nibble that has fascinated us for so long and made us fuse sin with pride. . . . We do not defy the gods by courageously stealing the fire from the celestial hearth. . . . Nothing so heroic. We fritter away our destiny by letting some snake tell us what to do.[26]

One of the feminist critiques of Niebuhr which was first published not long after *The Nature and Destiny of Man* and prior to Cox's interpretation takes a position similar to that of Cox, but for a different purpose. Valerie Saiving questions Niebuhr's emphasis on pride and will to power as the basic human sin because if humankind is really both male and female, it is important to recognize that

> the temptations of woman *as woman* are not the same as the temptations of man *as man,* and the specifically feminine forms of sin—"feminine" not because they are confined to women or because women are incapable of sinning in other ways but because they are outgrowths of the basic feminine character structure—have a quality which can never be encompassed by such terms as "pride" and "will-to-power." An adequate understanding of sin needs to take into account such items as triviality, distractibility, and diffuseness; lack of an organizing center or focus; dependence on others for one's own self-definition; tolerance at the expense of standards of excellence; inability to respect the boundaries of privacy; sentimentality, gossipy sociability, and mistrust of reason—in short, underdevelopment or negation of the self.[27]

The feminine dilemma is, according to Saiving, the opposite of the masculine; therefore, theology needs to "reconsider its estimate of the human condition and redefine its categories of sin and redemption in terms of feminine as well as masculine experience."

Another example of this, which may be seen as a further corrective for and complement to Niebuhr, is Mary Daly's understanding of sin as "false naming." The human problem, she argues, is expressed in two basic forms: (1) stealing what is our essentially human capacity, the power of naming, and (2) accepting being "defined" or "named" by another.[28] Daly uses the custom in patriarchal culture of naming the female by the male as the key image for the human problem. Self-naming, on the other hand, "symbolizes an activity in which the individual participates in Be-ing by be-ing her or his potential in a process which unfolds without constriction by any oppressive conditioning." Men sin in their projection of guilt upon women, an act which blocks the becoming not only of women but of men. Women sin through their internalization of blame and guilt, and their complicity in oppression.[29]

My concern in this discussion of Niebuhr and those who

correct and complement his position is to affirm that humankind sins both by over-valuing and under-valuing the self. The different reasons given for this seem to me to be considerably less important than the affirmation itself. We sin by claiming to be either more or less than we are, through pride or triviality, through naming or limiting another, and through allowing ourselves to be confined by the limitations others may place on us.

There are some obvious parallels between what Niebuhr says about the human condition and sin and what I have been saying about our defenses against shame. Power or powerlessness as a defense against shame is one dimension of the more general response to the anxiety of the human situation. Shame and anxiety are not the same thing, although some anxiety activates defense against the specific experience of shame. We become anxious, for example, when we anticipate the possibility of re-experiencing our shame. Anxiety, however, is a broader, more generic human experience which may anticipate shame or other intense emotional and self-involving reaction. As Niebuhr presents it, anxiety is the psychological dimension of the inescapable experience of being human.

The essential element in the defensive use of power in relationships between persons is the necessity of one person's being under or over the other. When power is used, there is some attempt to assert or take advantage, and this may be done from the position of power or powerlessness. That persons can and should differ in their actual power to accomplish particular things in their relationships is assumed here. To claim or use that power to control or subdue another is an expression of our sin because it denies the freedom of the other person in the interest of protecting or advancing ourselves. The vision of humanity that can be seen both in Niebuhr and Mary Daly is one in which human freedom is limited only by the Creator, not by the anxious and defensive efforts of other human beings. Essential humanity is accepting our likeness to other persons without having to claim advantages of either power or powerlessness in relation to them.

In Tom's case, this means claiming neither power nor powerlessness in relation to his parents. Expressed psychologically, it is his grandiose self giving way to a more realistic self, and grandiosity may be expressed through using either one's power or lack of it. Tom expressed it both ways. On the one hand, he had developed a pattern of using his feeling of being victimized by his parents' divorce to explain his feelings of inadequacy and to avoid responsibility for doing anything about them. On the other hand, as an injured party—one who had been hurt obviously by his father's leaving the home and more subtly by his mother's needing him as much as she did—Tom held the power to forgive. In his fantasy, at least, he held the power "to bind and to loose" (Matt. 18:18)—a power which, to become fully human, he needed to surrender.

In my experience as a pastoral counselor with Tom and with others, it has seemed evident that the Christian tradition in some of its more common expressions has tended to re-inforce the association of forgiveness with power. An interesting example of this view, in a nonreligious context, can be found in Hannah Arendt's quite sophisticated and often quoted secular analysis, *The Human Condition.* Although her discussion of human forgiveness comes as a part of an attempt to show the dignity of humankind in its capacity for reflective, meaningful action, in contrast to work as merely a means of production or "making a living," she sees the power of forgiveness as an important part of this. "Without being forgiven, released from the consequences of what we have done, our capacity to act would, as it were, be confined to one single deed from which we could never recover; we would remain the victims of its consequences forever." In her argument, Arendt makes reference to Jesus, not in faith, but as the "discoverer of the role of forgiveness in the realm of human affairs. . . . The fact," she notes apologetically, "that he made this discovery in a religious context and articulated in religious language is no reason to take it any less seriously in a strictly secular sense."[30]

[88]

Jesus maintains against the "scribes and pharisees" first that it is not true that only God has the power to forgive, and second that this power does not derive from God—as though God, not men, would forgive through the medium of human beings—but on the contrary must be mobilized by men toward each other before they can hope to be forgiven by God also.[31]

I return later to Arendt's understanding of forgiveness as a saving corrective to human action. Here I simply note her association of forgiveness with power and suggest that this supports the view that the association of power and forgiveness is a rather widespread assumption.

The New Testament scholar Krister Stendahl, to whom I referred earlier in the chapter on shame and the problem of human forgiveness, suggests that the whole emphasis on sin and forgiveness in the church grows out of something other than a correct interpretation of Paul. Stendahl argues that Paul in his writings exhibited "a rather robust conscience" and was little concerned with personal sin and guilt. It was interpretation of Paul beginning with Augustine, who, as Stendahl puts it, "may well have been one of the first to express the dilemma of the introspective conscience," that began the interpretation of justification as something related to individual sins and the need for forgiveness. "The Augustinian line leads into the Middle Ages and reaches its climax in the penitential struggle of an Augustinian monk, Martin Luther, and in his interpretation of Paul." Stendahl's argument concludes with the statement, "The West for centuries has wrongly surmised that the biblical writers were grappling with problems which no doubt are ours, but which never entered their consciousness."[32]

This interpretation of Paul certainly does not exhaust or abolish as unfounded the New Testament concern with forgiveness. It does suggest, however, the importance of looking at factors in addition to biblical and theological ones that may influence such issues. The emphasis on sin and forgiveness as central in Christian understanding placed the church in the power position of offering and/or mediating forgiveness to her members, whether it emphasizes the ordained priest or the priesthood of all believers. The power position of the Grand Inquisitor in Dostoevsky's *The Brothers Karamazov* is one of the classic illustrations of this. The Grand Inquisitor, who speaks to the Christ throughout the dialogue from his position of forgiving power, says at one point, "You gave us the right to loosen and to bind their shackles, and, of course, You cannot think of depriving us of that right now. Why, then, have You come to interfere with us now?"[33]

The church's practice of offering forgiveness from a position of power has re-inforced a human need to compensate for shame and a feeling of powerlessness by replicating that offering to persons who have wronged us. The forgiveness and power association is apparent in the way in which my counselees, whatever their religious tradition, feel that they have been supported in the association of forgiveness with power by Christian thought and practice. The fact that they seem to use this power defensively in order to deal with their shame suggests that, like all of us, they are sinners who, as Niebuhr and others insist, struggle to escape what they really are. Thus, a significant part of the problem with human forgiveness is its having been understood as a power which persons may possess. This fact, coupled with the destructive ways in which we are tempted to use our power, suggests that it is important to find a way to understand human forgiveness that is less associated with our defensiveness and sin.

Again, however, we are left with a number of questions. If, for example, rage is as important as the chapter suggests, what are the implications of this for pastoral care and counseling? Is what Kohut states about the therapeutic response directly applicable to less structured pastoral work? How is the church's tradition of mediating God's forgiveness for particular sins related to forgiveness between persons in special relation to each other? If, as I have argued here, the power to forgive the acts of another is more often than not used defensively, what is it that allows us to give up that defense? I defer the discussion of these and other questions, however, until the major elements in the problem with human forgiveness have been presented. The next element to be considered is the defense of being right, and the rage that is so often associated with it.

Notes

1. Kaufman, *Shame: The Power of Caring*, pp. 85-101.
2. In her popular book, *Peoplemaking* (Palo Alto, Calif.: Science and Behavior Books, 1972), Virginia Satir identifies blaming as one of several patterns of ineffective communication.
3. Heinz Kohut, "Narcissism and Narcissistic Rage," *The Psychoanalytic Study of the Child* 27 (New York: Quadrangle, 1972):379.
4. Ibid., pp. 377-78, 380, 386.
5. Ibid., pp. 386-87.
6. Ibid., p. 388.
7. Ibid., p. 392.
8. Ibid., pp. 391-92.
9. Kohut, *How Does Psychoanalysis Cure?* (Chicago: The University of Chicago Press, 1984), p. 78.
10. Kaufman, *Shame: The Power of Caring*, pp. 88-89.
11. W. W. Meissner, *The Paranoid Process* (New York and London: Jason Aronson, 1978), p. 144.
12. Ibid., pp. 409-11.
13. Rollo May, *Power and Innocence* (New York: W. W. Norton, 1972), pp. 95, 97.
14. Rollo May, *The Discovery of Being: Writings in Existential Psychology* (New York and London: W. W. Norton, 1983), p. 79.
15. Michael P. Nichols, *Family Therapy: Concepts and Methods* (New York and London: Gardner Press, 1984), p. 46.
16. Jay Haley, "Control in Brief Psychotherapy," *Archives of General Psychiatry* 4 (1961):139-53.
17. Nichols, *Family Therapy*, pp. 452-53.
18. Cf. Boszormenyi-Nagy and Spark, *Invisible Loyalties*, pp. 26-27 and Lynn Hoffman, *Foundations of Family Therapy* (New York: Basic Books, 1981), pp. 190-96.
19. Haley's book, *The Power Tactics of Jesus Christ and Other Essays* (New York: Discus/Avon, 1969) is an attempt to show how power is used in situations not usually defined as involving power. Jesus' relations to persons are examined psychologically, not in terms of their religious meaning, to show that Jesus unabashedly used power to manipulate and control people. One does not have to agree with all that Haley says to understand his point—which is also Rollo May's—that power is involved in every interpersonal situation.
20. Reinhold Niebuhr, *The Nature and Destiny of Man: A Christian Interpretation* (New York: Charles Scribner's Sons, 1955), pp. 182-83.
21. Ibid., p. 185.
22. Ibid., pp. 190-92.
23. Jürgen Moltmann, *Theology of Hope* (New York: Harper & Row, 1967), p. 22.

24. Harvey G. Cox, *On Not Leaving It to the Snake* (New York: Macmillan, 1967), p. xiii.

25. Brian W. Grant, *From Sin to Wholeness* (Philadelphia: The Westminster Press, 1982), pp. 22 and 29.

26. Cox, *On Not Leaving It to the Snake,* p. xiv.

27. Valerie Saiving, "The Human Situation: A Feminine Viewpoint," *The Nature of Man in Theological and Psychological Perspective* (New York: Harper & Brothers, 1960), p. 165.

28. Mary Daly, *Beyond God the Father* (Boston: Beacon Press, 1973), pp. 8 and 50.

29. Wanda Warren Berry, "Images of Sin and Salvation in Feminist Theology," *Anglican Theological Review,* vol. 50, no. 1, p. 32.

30. Hannah Arendt, *The Human Condition* (Chicago: The University of Chicago Press, 1958), pp. 236-37.

31. Ibid., p. 238.

32. Krister Stendahl, *Paul Among Jews and Gentiles* (Philadelphia: Fortress Press, 1976), pp. 85 and 95.

33. Fyodor Dostoevsky, *The Brothers Karamazov,* trans. Andrew H. MacAndrew (New York: Bantam Books, 1981), p. 303.

Defending Against Shame with Righteousness

F orgive us our sins—*that we may discover the irrelevance of our righteousness.*

Perhaps the most familiar experience of a pastor or marital therapist beginning to work with a couple is hearing of the righteousness of one or both of the spouses. If only he hadn't done such and such, everything would have been fine. For the pastor who because of decision or circumstance begins counseling with only one member of a couple, the most likely thing that he or she will hear is how bad the absent spouse is and how unjustly the spouse who is present has been wronged.[1] Persons who question a significant other's caring for them are quite likely to retreat into righteousness. They deal with their shame by searching for the other's guilt.

As I have attempted to show earlier in the book, shame and guilt tend to appear together and are often confused with each other. Guilt is more behavioral and responsive to reason. It is, therefore, more manipulatable and manageable. In the midst of shame and injury to one's self, which is essentially unmanageable, searching out the guilt of the one who has contributed to one's shame appears to be something that *can* be done. And as most pastors can attest, it is often done with great zeal. In my office it is not unusual for a person who has been shamed by some sort of infidelity to pace up and down the room rather than sit calmly in a chair.

I have debated the appropriateness of my use of the term *righteousness* for this defense against further shame and injury to the self. The term *righteousness,* although not archaic, is certainly not in common usage where I live and work, and when it is used it is generally used negatively to categorize and dismiss certain people from serious consideration because they are "self-righteous." What I mean by the defense of righteousness may include that negative designation but is intended not as a dismissal. Rather it is a call for investigation of a profound human phenomenon—the need to be right in order to protect oneself from what is experienced as a threat of destruction.

Righteousness is defensive when it is a response to shame and an attack upon one's self. This was the case with Emmie, whose husband, Elmer, had simply left her without saying anything. He never told her why, although she could think about many possible reasons. Whatever the reasons, Emmie, who had always been a family woman, was now an abandoned woman—left, it seemed, only with her shame. She did not call it shame; but the fact that Elmer never gave her a reason or reasons sent her the message that there was something inadequate about who and what she was.

Emmie was different from many people whose marriages terminate and who feel at least as much guilt as shame. The wife whose husband made it very clear that he was leaving because of her failure to control her weight had something specific to feel guilty about. Similarly, the husband who was unable to manage money provided his wife with a specific reason why life with him looked like it would always be a struggle with debt and bankruptcy. There was obvious guilt as well as shame in both of these situations, and because there was something obvious for each of these persons to feel guilty about, the guilt gave some relief from their shame. Thus, the attack upon the self was not as radical as it might otherwise have been. Emmie, however, had nothing specific, no obvious guilt to draw her away from the more diffuse pain of her self-injury. What she did, as I interpret her situation, was to give attention to her husband's guilt, contrasting it with her righteousness until, as I observed it, she could discover guilt of her own.

Emmie's primary defense against shame and self-injury was the "fact" that she was in the right. She was the injured party who had done no wrong. I place the word *fact* in quotation marks to suggest some of the difficulty in dealing with an issue such as this one on a supposedly factual basis. When I first entered the ministry, according to the *Discipline* of the Methodist Church, it was my responsibility to determine the guilt or innocence of divorced persons seeking to be married again. I was expected to determine the "facts" of the case and act accordingly because it was thought to be appropriate for the church to marry "innocent persons," but not to marry those judged to be guilty of violating the marriage contract. Likewise, most divorce actions attempted in some way to redress an injury. Both the church and the legal system encouraged persons to respond to the situation of separation and divorce by proclaiming their innocence and trying to demonstrate the guilt of another.

Although the practice of having to prove innocence to an external judge still exists in some churches, in my own it does not. The official reasons for proving innocence to an ecclesiastical judge no longer exist. The United Methodist Church and a number of others have attempted to take their clergy out of the business of making judgments of innocence or guilt in such cases. Moreover, the majority of states now have some kind of "no-fault" divorce law which allows one party to obtain a divorce on the basis of his or her own judgment that the marriage is "irretrievably broken," and one party's fault in breaking the marriage contract no longer has to be proved. In the absence of these external reasons for proving innocence, however, the phenomenon continues because internal reasons for proving innocence continue to be in effect. Demonstrating that one is in the right with respect to the marriage or other circumstance where one has been shamed and that, more broadly, one is a good person are important defenses against further injury to the self.

Righteousness as Innocence

One of the more common claims of righteousness, particularly as this is set over against the guilt of another, is the affirmation of innocence. Rollo May's analysis of innocence is useful as a beginning point for understanding righteousness as a defense against shame. He distinguishes between two kinds of innocence. "One is innocence as a quality of the imagination, the innocence of the poet or artist. . . . It is the preservation of childlike attitudes into maturity without sacrificing the realism of one's perception of evil." The other type of innocence is that for which the prototype is Melville's Billy Budd. It is a pseudo-innocence, a naïveté which consists in a childishness rather than childlikeness. "With unconscious purpose we close our eyes to reality and persuade ourselves that we have escaped it."[2]

Pseudo-innocence for May is a denial of power and, with it, responsibility. "We cannot develop responsibility for what we don't admit we have. . . . As a nation," he says, "America has . . . failed to develop a viable sense of tragedy, which would serve, through making for empathy with our enemies, to mitigate our cruelty." He quotes appreciatively Henry Steele Commager's comment: "Two world wars have not induced in (Americans) either a sense of sin or that awareness of evil almost instinctive with Old World peoples" and concludes, "Innocence as a shield from responsibility is also a shield from growth. It protects us from new awareness and from identifying with the sufferings of mankind as well as with the joys."[3]

For my purposes innocence can be understood as a dimension of the defense of righteousness in that the proclamation that one is right carries with it a claim of "no fault" and lack of responsibility for whatever has happened. This was Emmie's claim during much of her counseling with me. It was Elmer who had broken the marriage and had been unreliable for much of the time prior to that. If it were not for him, everything would be all right. If anything had been wrong in their marriage and with her, she was certainly unaware of it.

Sheldon Kopp's *End to Innocence* addresses the problem of pseudo-innocence in a way that has been useful both to my counselees and to my students. Although he does not operate from within a Christian framework, his realism about persons and the world is in many ways akin to that of Reinhold Niebuhr. He insists early in his book that denying the destructiveness in ourselves and others "turns us toward easy and unwitting complicity with evil," and in a classic chapter, "Pollyanna and the Paranoid," pointedly caricatures these apparently opposite ways of avoiding the discomfort of reality, both of which should be familiar to pastors.

Kopp attacks the classic position of the psychotherapy patient who feels that he or she is something special or that what has happened to him or her justifies unusual attention. This view of specialness is a way of isolating oneself from other people. It is one example of an oversimplified view of the world. The paranoid and the Pollyanna attitudes are variations of the specialness theme: one claiming that I have the worst of everything; the other claiming that I have the best. "Believing that things usually turn out bad is as naïve as believing that this is the best of all possible worlds. An overly optimistic Pollyanna attitude is simply a more obvious form of pseudo-innocence than a cynically paranoid outlook." Kopp further caricatures the Pollyanna attitude by calling it "*narapoia*—an inverted form of paranoia." His description of the narapoid is in many ways applicable to Emmie and her relationship to Elmer.

> The more coldly detached their lovers, the more trustingly narapoids cling to them. Some of these patients are men, but most are women. Our male-dominated culture does much to maintain its sexist power structure by selectively encouraging women to believe in this particular brand of pseudo-innocence.[4]

Kopp advocates the rereading of Lewis Carroll's *Alice's Adventures in Wonderland* as means of ending our innocence.

"The failure of Alice's literal attempts to learn the rules for the order of things in lawless Wonderland vicariously guides the reader along the inevitably futile parallel and metaphoric search for meaning in his or her own life." Familiar conventions of social exchange and language do not work in Wonderland. It is a place

> where the everyday assumptions on which we usually depend turn out to be empty illusions that do not warrant our innocent attachment to them. . . .
>
> Once Alice can no longer count on her beliefs making sense, she finds that along with her loss of security, she loses her identity. The same painfully perplexing question echoes throughout her adventures: "But then . . . who am I?" . . .
>
> . . . Alice's difficulties culminate in a final test of Wonderland's rules, in an irreverent courtroom scene in which "the Law" itself is on trial! For Alice underground and above-ground courts turn out to be too much alike. . . .
>
> Both systems of justice are incoherent and unfair. This similarity threatens Alice with the near realization that her own everyday world is just as chaotic a combination of anarchy and artifice as this terrifying subterranean nightmare.[5]

Alice's adventures have often been likened to a dream which in its distortion of reality underscores the pain of a reality which is difficult to face. Kopp is insisting that the world of Alice's Wonderland is not that different from the way things really are. It is a reality that my counselee, Emmie, had been avoiding most of her life with something like the Pollyanna stance. Her recent experience of shame, however, had moved her closer to the Paranoid position in this two-part caricature. Both positions provide ways of avoiding responsibility. Her initial rage and claim of innocence echoed the words heard so often by parents from their children and also constantly expressed in the less inspirational but perhaps more human parts of the Psalms: "It's not fair!" Kopp's mission seems to be to help his patients and readers accept that fact. His contribution to Christians can be particularly significant because of a realism about life that can allow us to see the good news about humankind, which Kopp does not see, without

Pollyanna's blinders in a world that is often unfair and essentially unexplainable.

Righteousness Through Blaming

Another dimension of the defense of righteousness is the ability to blame others for whatever predicament one is in. In response to the shame that one feels or anticipates and which seems to focus all attention upon oneself, the claim of being in the right depends on the ability to locate the problem elsewhere. In *Pastoral Counseling: A Ministry of the Church,* I presented the issue of determining the degree to which a person locates his or her pain internally or externally as one of the important questions in pastoral diagnosis.[6] It is a good test of the prognosis of a particular situation. The person who can locate "the problem" at least to some degree within himself or herself is much more likely to be successful in the counseling process. Blaming attempts to avoid the shame of being seen as faulty or inadequate by focusing responsibility for one's predicament on someone else. As Gershen Kaufman puts it:

> The person who maintains his or her righteousness by blaming perceives the source of all that goes wrong to lie outside the self, and, paradoxically, beyond internal control. And though that individual resents the resulting feeling of powerlessness, a powerlessness to affect and change what ails him, he never recognizes that he has colluded in the very process of creating that powerlessness. . . . If the source of what goes wrong in life becomes external to the self, one has . . . relinquished the power to affect or alter what happens.[7]

Many examples of the defenses both of righteousness and of power may be found in Eric Berne's discussion of psychological games, which became popular about twenty years ago. "A game," according to Berne, "is an ongoing series of complementary ulterior transactions progressing to a well-defined, predictable outcome."[8] Games serve to call attention away from oneself and one's own responsibility by concentrating on the stereotypical rules of the game. The protagonist in all of Berne's games is called "White," indicating that at least one of the purposes of all of these interpersonal games is good's winning out over externalized evil or, more simply, developing a rationale for blaming another for one's predicament. Virtually any means is justified to win out over one's opponent. Thus, most of the games have a strong power element as well as a polarization of right and wrong.

An example of a game in which the payoff is both power and righteousness is the game which Berne calls "Now I've Got You, You Son of a Bitch." To illustrate this game, Berne takes the familiar situation of an agreement between a homeowner and a plumber for a repair job in the home. The price is set, and both agree that there will be no extras.

> When the plumber submitted his bill, he included a few dollars extra for an unexpected valve that had to be installed—about four dollars on four-hundred dollar job. White became infuriated, called the plumber on the phone and demanded an explanation. The plumber would not back down. White wrote him a long letter criticizing his integrity and ethics and refused to pay the bill until the extra charge was withdrawn. The plumber finally gave in.[9]

As Berne interprets it, in this particular game both White and the plumber are aware that they are playing games. The awareness, however, is clearly in the background and can be recognized only when someone calls it to their attention or when they shift their awareness from the game mentality. The innocent, unaware person is protecting himself from the evils of those who would take advantage of him. The key to this particular illustration is the satisfaction in having the plumber in the wrong. While on the surface this was a legitimate business dispute, White now felt justified in venting almost unlimited rage against this evil and dishonest person.

Only slightly hidden, however, was the power agenda—using the opportunity of the mistake to "make criticisms of the plumber's whole way of living." What seems crucial for our purposes is noting the now-I've-got-you satisfaction which the transgression of the agreement brings to the "injured" party. The personal familiarity that I myself have with this game suggests to me that it may be quite familiar to the reader as well.

Shifting the focus of our attention to the special relations of the family, in my experience as a pastoral counselor I have seen more "injured" parties than I would want to count responding to the infidelity of their spouse with something comparable to the satisfaction of White to the four-dollar plumbing mistake. Again, Berne is instructive in his naming of the game "Now I've Got You. . . ." The implication is that the particular injury may be less important than the old injuries of the past. It is simply evidence of what the injured party had thought all along. Complicating this in a marriage where divorce is contemplated is the concept of the injured party which has been supported by both church and state. In states with so-called no-fault divorce laws there still appears to be some advantage in demonstrating how bad the other party is in order to exact a more advantageous settlement. Even when there is little or no actual possibility of such an outcome, the fantasy remains that the legal system will help the injured party punish the other. Sometimes it does, but much less often than the fantasy suggests.

This discussion illustrates how closely the defenses of power and of righteousness are related to each other. Being right appears to give power to compensate for the shame which one has experienced. My concern here, however, has been to focus upon how being the injured party offers power over the injuring one through the withholding of forgiveness. Josh, for example, knows that his wife has had an affair, but she does not know that he knows. Or at least he thinks that she does not know that he knows. As I recall the situation, I do not remember whether she knows that he knows or not, probably because I think it doesn't matter. As Josh talks with me about the situation, he seems to have a mixture of sadness about the affair and pleasure in knowing about it to help him feel more righteous than his wife, Jean. Interestingly, if I were to suggest to him that he forgive

Jean, I would most likely be supporting him in his position of power over her. Only at the point that Josh seemed close to seeing his sin as well as Jean's did it become possible to confront him with his self-serving use of the power to forgive.

Righteousness as Perfectionism

In addition to innocence or pseudo-innocence, perfectionism is another dimension of the defense of righteousness. Perfectionism "is a striving against shame and attempts to compensate for an underlying sense of defectiveness. If I can become perfect, no longer am I so vulnerable to shame."[10] In his discussion of defenses against shame, Gershen Kaufman makes use of Karen Horney's discussion of perfectionism as one of the "expansive solutions" to the uncertainy about one's self-worth. Horney does not mention shame, but shame is implied as one of those elements in an inadequate self that the perfection is trying to avoid. Such a person, according to Horney,

> feels superior because of his high standards, moral and intellectual, and on this basis looks down on others. His arrogant contempt for others, though, is hidden—from himself as well—behind polished friendliness, because his very standards prohibit such "irregular" feelings.[11]

Horney feels that the obvious, behavioral elements of perfectionism are only its superficial aspects. "What really matters is not those petty details but the flawless excellence of the whole conduct of life." The perfectionist moves beyond behavior to "equate in his mind standards and actualities—*knowing* about moral values and *being* a good person." Such persons may expect others to live up to their moral values at the same time that they are deceiving themselves about their own ability to do so. The perfectionist as described by Horney can be placed in a state of panic when confronted by the revelation of Alice's Wonderland that life is not fair.

Because he is fair, just, dutiful, he is entitled to fair treatment by others and by life in general. This conviction of an infallible justice operating in life gives him a feeling of mastery. His own perfection therefore is not only a means to superiority but also one to control life. The idea of undeserved fortune, whether good or bad, is alien to him. . . . He not only resents ill fortune as unfair but, over and beyond this, . . . it invalidates his whole accounting system and conjures up the ghastly prospect of helplessness.[12]

The Case of Herman and Hilda

These words from Horney are a fairly accurate description of Herman, an accountant for a large company who came to me for pastoral counseling because of his rage toward his wife, Hilda. She had been unfaithful to him, and Herman reported that he just couldn't bear looking at her because of his lack of respect for her. He had felt this way, he said, for the last six months. As I got to know Herman in that first meeting I discovered that he held an office in his United Methodist church which placed him on virtually every church committee. He was constantly going to meetings. His commitment to the church, quite appropriately, gained him great admiration from the other church members, and in addition to his church duties he was a Scoutmaster and also was involved in coaching activities for young people. He had irrefutable evidence that he was a "good man," and the respect of the community to prove it beyond the shadow of a doubt.

I pointed out to Herman in our first session together that his "goodness" was a problem, and somewhat to my surprise, he seemed to understand. As I tried to interpret to him what I had heard, I commented that a marriage between a "good" man and a "bad" woman was hardly a marriage because one partner always had something on the other. If I were to help at all with the marriage, it would involve discovering some of his badness and his wife's goodness. Although I did not claim that his "affair" with the church was as bad as his wife's affair with another man, I did suggest that they might have some of the same qualities, and that we would have to explore them together.

The point here is not to discuss a technique of working with troubled marriages, but to illustrate the use of some very good activities as a defense against strong feelings of inadequacy and a fragile sense of self. My attempt in the first session was to begin my communication with Herman by suggesting that pastoral counseling would be dealing with more than his rage toward Hilda. It would involve the gradual dismantling of his perfectionism and the discovery of how the good things he did might be used to avoid even more important issues of his life.

It was certainly not clear at the beginning, but it soon became evident that Herman's shame over Hilda's infidelity was related to his own shame over his own inadequacy as a dependable provider for his family. Gershen Kaufman's words seem accurately to describe what he had been experiencing.

> . . . an individual already burdened by a deep, abiding sense of defectiveness will strive to erase every blemish of the self and experiences an inordinate pressure to excel in an ever-widening circle of activities. Since one already knows that one is inherently not good enough as a person, nothing one does is ever seen as sufficient, adequate, or good enough. . . . shamefulness requires that awareness of difference between self and other becomes automatically translated into a comparison of good versus bad, better versus worse. An individual already carrying shame reacts to such awareness of difference by engaging actively, though wholly internally, in a form of comparison-making, comparing himself to the other who is seen as different in some essential way.[13]

It is striking how accurately what Kaufman has to say about perfectionism describes what I observed and responded to in pastoral counseling with Herman and Hilda.

Righteousness and Rage

Another valuable perspective in understanding both Emmie's and Herman's defenses against shame is that of psychiatrist Mardi Horowitz. As a part of his investigations of psychological states of mind, he has studied the state of self-righteous rage—the state most evident in Emmie and Herman. "Most people," says Horowitz, "have moments of God-like wrath, usually restricted to fantasy, in which devastation of others is justified by their evil qualities."[14] This kind of rage "is often triggered by injuries to the self-concept" and involves a "destructive readiness to injure others on the grounds that they have no right to survive if the self is diminished."

What Horowitz calls "self-righteous rage" is very close in meaning to Kohut's concept of narcissistic rage which I discussed in chapter 3. In fact, what Horowitz says about self-righteous rage can be understood as a complement to Kohut's views. The differences occur primarily at the point of what each theory attempts to accomplish. Horowitz is attempting to develop a systematic description of states of mind in order to have an accurate way of describing change in psychotherapy. Kohut's concern is in developing a psychoanalytic theory which is based primarily upon psychological phenomena rather than on concepts drawn from physics.

A state of mind, as Horowitz describes it, is "a recurrent pattern of experience and of behavior that is both verbal and nonverbal." "State description is a way of condensing multiple observations into a limited set of patterns."[15] In focusing upon the particular qualities of the state of mind in self-righteous rage, Horowitz is able to contrast this particular state with other responses to shame and self-injury, such as "the mixed state of shame-rage-anxiety," a "chronic embitterment state," and a state of "withdrawn, numb, apathetic dullness." He notes that self-righteous rage often seems to be preferred to these other states because it removes a person from "experiencing life at a deadened level," and he illustrates this with the description of a patient's rage toward his wife, which was precipitated by her botching a home improvement project. When the patient described the event at the next analytic session, he accompanied it with a matter-of-fact statement about her clumsiness and a vague reference to his discomfort when she became sullen. In his demeanor and style he showed his characteristic *chronically embittered* state. His voice had a hard, biting edge as he spoke contemptuously of his wife. He did not communicate all of the details of the event, but focused instead on describing her ineptitude. . . . While doing so, he relived the state of *self-righteous rage*. His voice became full-bodied, with strong, angry exclamatory tones.[16]

The interesting point about this description is the apparent "enjoyment" of self-righteous rage as a choice over more ego-controlled states because of the sense of vitality it offers. In the therapeutic process, according to Horowitz, resistance may increase as a result of insight into one's pattern of rage. The liveliness of rage can extricate a person "from the states of *apathetic dullness* so common in narcissistically vulnerable persons." In fact, rages can be idealized, and like an old friend, "embraced to avoid further loss."[17] Put in an oversimplified and perhaps caricatured way, it feels better to be angry than depressed, particularly if the rage one feels is *justified*.

The means of justifying that rage can be quite elaborate. In order to develop a more inclusive theoretical base than can be provided through the use of the psychoanalytic terms *superego* and *ego ideal,* Horowitz presents a scenario of how rage is justified by using some of the work of Joseph Campbell, who is best known for his extensive study of the structure and function of myth in human life and culture. In an early work, *The Hero with a Thousand Faces,* Campbell describes some of the forms of the hero story that repeatedly appears in our dreams and in the myths and fairy tales of many cultures. Although the variety in form is striking, the common features of these stories are even more striking. One of the problems with the analysis, viewed twenty years later, is its sexism—the fact that virtually all the heroes are male, and females appear primarily as prizes or temptations.

In his scenario (greatly simplified here), Campbell describes the universal hero as receiving a call to do a great and important deed. He battles fierce odds, dragons, monsters, forces of evil, etc., overcomes them, and returns home bearing boons. Usually he is received with honor, but sometimes he is unappreciated and rejected as having become a foreigner or one contaminated by an alien culture. In the midst of all its variations, we can discern in this story someone of worth and dignity with whom to identify and circumstances of importance which can make the events of our lives seem more important. Our identification with the hero's journey is largely an unconscious one, but it can often be discerned as we think about the trials that we face in the course of our lives. We do not have "to risk the adventure alone; for the heroes of all time have gone before us; the labyrinth is thoroughly known; we have only to follow the thread of the hero-path."[18] There are strong similarities in the stories of Campbell's hero and such dissimilar protagonists as Berne's White, Paul's picture of his struggle with principalities and powers, and the efforts of our parishioners and ourselves to defend ourselves against shame.

In describing the self-justifying fantasies of self-righteous rage, Horowitz simplifies the hero story to three roles: the hero, the monster, and the critical audience. The hero, in this case one whose self has been injured, is fighting an evil force or person in order to prevent re-injury and, in fantasy it seems, to save others from similar injury by the monster. What Horowitz brings out in his analysis is that this fight goes on as if in an arena—before a critical audience whose approval is the reward for the hero's efforts. The audience in the hero stories may be the community from which the hero goes out on his quest, a parent, a great king, or a god. The important point is that just as shame occurred by one's being seen by that critical audience as weak or rejected, vindication comes through proving oneself to that same audience.

The critic admires the hero and loathes the monster. In this situation the hero may exhibit a *self-righteous rage* state. The three-party role structure is useful here in understanding why a usually restrained person, when confronted with triggers that instigate this model, may freely express fierce, brutal, but pleasurably exciting hostility. The pleasure is an assumption of dominance over a dehumanized other, a pleasure heightened by feelings of merger with a powerful critic (or group) to gain attention, admiration, and praise.[19]

This three-role theory is complementary with Kohut's understanding of narcissistic rage in that it adds an image of the thought process in rage to a developmental rationale of the psychology of the self. Pleasing that audience is to be achieved at all costs and through the use of the most effective methods available. The qualities of the audience or critic vary according to the individual fantasy of the justifying person. The more unrealistic versions of the critic, according to Horowitz,

> may attribute good only according to grandiose standards of perfection, with sadistic devaluation of everything that falls short of these standards. . . . The harsher and more pathologically idealistic and grandiose the critic's role, the greater the tendency to the dehumanizing and explosive variants of *self-righteous rage*.[20]

Horowitz's adaptation of Campbell's work to the interpretation of self-righteous rage is valuable at a number of points. The hero image provides another way to interpret the self-preoccupation of the narcissistically injured person. The response to his or her injury, in fantasy at least, becomes a cause or a quest. Monsters like the injuring person need to be stamped out. No ground should be given. No attempt to see things from the monster's point of view can be tolerated. Moreover, the injured person indeed seems to be playing a role, in that deviations from that role cannot be tolerated. Resistance to new data and insights in the counseling process can often be understood as resistance to deviation from the hero's righteous role. This is accentuated by the sense that the person is playing to an audience which evaluates his or her performance in terms of faithfulness to the role. Feelings which might cause role deviation might also cause the critic to forget who is the hero and who is the monster.

Emmie's resistance to seeing any good in Elmer and her trying vainly to keep her children from seeing any can certainly be interpreted in terms of the three-role scheme. Her defense against the shame she felt caused her to rigidify the roles she saw herself and Elmer playing in their marriage. His role required that all the bad things be attributed to him. Her claim to the righteous or hero role was not so much in the good things that she had done, but in what she perceived to be a fact—that she had not done any really bad things. She reacted to her children's involvement with Elmer as if it were a betrayal of her and thus revealed her belief that, as in the story of hero and monster, if someone wins the other has to lose. Her children were a part of the critical audience she was playing to, and she had to compensate for her shame at rejection by winning their approval.

The kind of rage that I have been discussing is more than a feeling, but a "feeling state" or state of mind continuing over a period of time. What the self has done to protect itself from the experience of shame has become disconnected from the original source of the shame experience and become a generalized reaction to many different stimuli. It has become a state of mind or what Horowitz in his research has defined as "a recurrent pattern of experience or behavior that is both verbal and nonverbal. . . . Any person's states and patterns of state transition are the behavioral manifestations of his character structure or personality."[21] In Gershen Kaufman's theory, what has happened with the rage is that it has become internalized along with shame as a strategy of defense. It is "no longer one affect or feeling among many which all become activated and then pass on. Rage is actively held onto and thereby prolonged, whether expressed or only felt inside."[22]

In the case of Emmie, the intensity of the rage, its duration, and the inability of improving external circumstances in her life to change her feelings in any significant way make a strong case for the presence of early narcissistic injury. In contrast to her predominantly passive and accepting style of life, there was in Emmie throughout most of our relationship what Kohut has described as "the need for revenge, for righting a wrong, for undoing a hurt by whatever means, and a deeply anchored, unrelenting compulsion in the pursuit of all these aims." The intensity of such rage in this quiet little woman was striking, and the fact that all my efforts to deal directly and somewhat rationally with her husband's recent rejection of her were unsuccessful gives further evidence that the recent shame caused by her husband's leaving reactivated an injury to her self which occurred much earlier in life.

I was not consciously offering Emmie pastoral counseling that was based on Kohut's self-psychology. I am interpreting the case after the fact in the light of theoretical insights which seem to me to help understand what was going on. What I did do, however, was not inconsistent with that theory. On reflection now, what a clearer awareness of self-psychology and the phenomenon of narcissistic rage might have done was to help me be more realistic about the depth of change that was needed. I was in the position of the impatient disciples who came to Jesus unable to cast out a demon and to whom some manuscripts record him as saying: "This kind never comes out except by prayer and fasting" (Matt. 17:21). A narcissistic injury is usually a prayer-and-fasting case—one that may require all the extra help one can get. Perhaps most important, Emmie's experience is a valuable reminder that with the problem of human forgiveness, it is usually inadequate simply to address the immediate injury. A long, patient ministry to the whole person may be required. Not just her rejection by her husband, but her whole life was the issue at hand.

Emmie's primary defense against the shame which she experienced was her righteousness or innocence of any offense. One of the difficulties with righteousness as a defense is the fact that one's religion is expected to contribute to one's righteousness and the doing of good things on behalf of others. One of the difficulties of dealing with Herman's rage toward Hilda or Emmie's toward Elmer was that it was "self-righteous" or "justified" rage. Consciously they had come to a pastoral counselor trying to find a way to give up this rage and forgive those who had wronged them. Unconsciously they were holding on to their rage because it helped defend themselves against the shame they had experienced because of their vulnerable self-structure. Moreover, their religious beliefs seemed to support them in their righteous defenses of themselves against shame.

Religion and Righteousness

Although the justification of oneself through being right is popularly understood to be supported by religion, righteousness in both Old and New Testaments has more to do with relationship than with right behavior. In contrast to this biblical view, righteousness as it is popularly understood is more like the practice of determining who is innocent in a divorce situation than it is based upon a Christian understanding. In the Old Testament, righteousness "is a thoroughly Hebraic concept, foreign to the Western mind and at variance with the common understanding of the term." It "is not behavior in accordance with an ethical, legal, psychological, religious, or spiritual norm" or "giving every man his just due." Righteousness in the Old Testament is "the fulfillment of the demands of a relationship, whether that relationship be with men or with God." "The covenant relation was prior to all law and all demands. Yahweh had chosen Israel. That was the basic fact of her existence. . . . Faith is the fulfillment of the relationship to Yahweh and is thereby righteousness" (Gen. 15:6; Hab. 2:4).[23]

In order to understand the Old Testament concept of righteousness, according to Pedersen, "we must go back to the fundamental psychological conception." Righteous action "is created by the whole of the soul; the more the whole of the soul is implied, the more it acts in accordance with its nature. . . . The integrity of the soul is therefore an expression of its righteousness. . . . A *pure* heart . . . is the same as a whole heart, for it implies a soul the integrity of which is not broken by foreign wills or contaminating elements. The opposite is a divided heart (Ps. 12:3)."

> To act rightly is not to act according to rules which are forced upon the man from without. The good man acts rightly, because he acts entirely in accordance with the nature of his soul. But the soul exists only as a link in a covenant; it maintains its nature by maintaining the covenant. . . . Israelitic psychology does not distinguish between ability and will. The healthy soul is that which is able to act according to its nature.[24]

Pederson states that the righteous person "is always 'whole' with those with whom he has entered upon a covenant" and that righteousness "manifests itself in love, because it consists in maintaining the covenant."

The use of the concept of "righteousness" in the New Testament also presumes a concept of covenant relationship,

> which, for its preservation, needs the active participation of both covenant partners. Thus, the one who upholds, and therefore participates in, this covenant relationship is designated "righteous"; and, as in the OT, those acts which preserve a covenant relationship, either between God and man, or between man and man, are righteous, while those acts which break this relationship are unrighteous.[25]

Although there are other ways in which the concept of righteousness is used, in the New Testament it is most often the "trusting acceptance of God's saving act in Christ, whereby man accepts the restored covenant relationship with God."[26] In both testaments, then, righteousness is understood as an expression of the whole soul or person—rather than as particular acts in accordance with an external law—and as an expression of the relatedness of persons in the covenant with God and with one another.

If faith in God's relationship with us is the proper understanding of righteousness in the Bible, then why is righteousness so often identified with being right, innocent, or good? Because there is a deep human need to explain one's affirmation by God and other human beings in terms other than election or grace. The counterpoint in scripture and in life between law and grace tends to be undermined by the human need for certainty and the difficulty of maintaining faith in something like God's covenant with his people that is essentially unexplainable. Whereas Christian rightness with God means rightly related or in communion with God and one's brothers and sisters in the faith, being able to trust that relationship as enough remains a constant human problem.

The problem is accentuated when a person has suffered injury to the self and has experienced shame. Not unlike the way in which the Hebrew people seemed to struggle with the issue of how they could be God's elect and at the same time suffer so much shame and disgrace, individuals who have been rejected and feel shamed by that rejection find it almost impossible to have faith in their continuing favor with God and with others. What occurs—as it did with Emmie—is an attempt to *prove* what no longer can be accepted in faith. The fantasy of the hero and the monster emerges, and the hero must prove his or her integrity by defeating the representation of evil before the audience, which can pronounce him or her justified.

Jesus' discussion of the so-called "higher righteousness" in the Sermon on the Mount can be instructive here. The message of the familiar verse, "For I tell you, unless your righteousness exceeds that of the scribes and Pharisees, you will never enter the kingdom of heaven" (Matt. 5:20), must have been presented at a time when the scribes and Pharisees were declining in their influence and power.[27] In this context their need to prove themselves and their religion was more evident than in earlier times when they had more significant influence within their society. The Pharisee of Jesus' parable thanking God that he was not as other men were can be understood as making a defensive statement in a particular social situation of diminishing positive identity and power. It is also prototypical for all persons who have felt shame and loss of community and identity. Their righteousness becomes a substitute for what they have lost.

[113]

In that sense, righteousness as a defense develops not so much out of certainty about one's religion as uncertainty about it. The righteousness that "exceeds that of the scribes and Pharisees" develops out of having a strong sense of self, of who one is, and having faith that that identity is true. Not unlike the Israelitic psychology which Pedersen describes, Augustine points out that the Christian is not the person who struggles to do the good and to prove himself or herself righteous in doing so. Rather, the Christian is one for whom the good has become an expression of who he or she is through grace. "By faith comes the obtaining of grace against sin; by grace comes the healing of the soul from sin's sickness; by the healing of the soul comes freedom of choice; by freedom of choice comes the love of righteousness."[28] It is in the light of this affirmation that we can interpret Jesus' parable of the Last Judgment in Matthew 28. Those on the Father's right hand were unaware of the righteous things which they had done. They had apparently done them as a natural part of the healing they had received through grace.

The meaning of this "higher righteousness," in contrast to defensive righteousness, can be discussed more adequately as a part of the final two chapters of this book. Similar to the defense of power, righteousness which is sought or claimed to prove something can be seen as a substitute for relationship or as a lack of faith that significant relationship to God and one's fellow human beings can really exist. For both Emmie and Herman, righteousness was a defense against shame which focused upon the guilt of those who had hurt them rather than their being unable to find their own.

The questions left us at the end of this chapter have to do with a number of issues. For example, if, as I have suggested, righteousness used defensively is a significant part of the problem with human forgiveness, at what point, if any, does it become a positive part of a relationship? How is it to be judged and by whom? If rage is experienced as an alternative to depression or other less satisfying psychological states, is there a way in which its counterproductive elements can be avoided? If it is important for a narcissistically injured person to surrender his or her righteousness, in what way does pastoral counseling facilitate this? If, as was suggested in the case of Herman and Hilda, there is such a thing as a balance of "goodness" in a marriage or family, what are the optimum conditions for this balance? These and other questions need to be addressed, but they should be deferred until after the discussion of some of the problems in understanding human forgiveness itself.

Notes

1. See chapters 4 and 5 of my book *Pastoral Counseling: A Ministry of the Church* (Nashville: Abingdon Press, 1983) for some ideas about structuring the pastoral counseling of couples which may make these early sessions more useful.

2. Rollo May, *Power and Innocence* (New York: W. W. Norton, 1972), pp. 43-44.

3. Ibid., pp. 47, 48, 58.

4. Sheldon Kopp, *An End to Innocence: Facing Life Without Illusions* (New York: Bantam Books, 1978). p. 95.

5. Ibid., pp. 165-66.

6. Patton, *Pastoral Counseling: A Ministry*, pp. 140-43.

7. Kaufman, *Shame: The Power of Caring*, p. 95.

8. Eric Berne, *Games People Play: The Psychology of Human Relationships* (New York: Grove Press, 1964), p. 48.

9. Ibid., p. 85.

10. Kaufman, *Shame: The Power of Caring*, p. 90.

11. Karen Horney, *Neurosis and Human Growth* (New York: W. W. Norton, 1950), p. 196.

12. Ibid., p. 197.

13. Kaufman, *Shame: The Power of Caring*, p. 90.

14. Mardi J. Horowitz, "Self-Righteous Rage and the Attribution of Blame," *Archives of General Psychiatry* 38 (November 1981): 1233.

15. Mardi J. Horowitz, *States of Mind: Analysis of Change in Psychotherapy* (New York and London: Plenum Medical Book Co., 1979), pp. 30-31.

16. Horowitz, "Self-Righteous Rage," p. 1234.

17. Ibid, p. 1237.

18. Joseph Campbell, *The Hero with a Thousand Faces* (New York: Meridian Books, 1956), p. 25.

19. Horowitz, "Self-Righteous Rage," p. 1235.

20. Ibid., p. 1236.

21. Horowitz, *States of Mind*, pp. 31-32.

22. Kaufman, *Shame: The Power of Caring*, p. 86.

23. E. R. Achtemeier, "Righteousness in the OT," *Interpreter's Dictionary of the Bible* R–Z:80, 82.

24. Pedersen, *Israel: Its Life and Culture,* pp. 336-38.
25. P. J. Achtemeier, "Righteousness in the NT," *IDB* R–Z:91.
26. Ibid.
27. Matthew Black, "Pharisees," *IDB* K–Q: 780.
28. Augustine, "The Spirit and the Letter," in *Augustine: Later Works,* trans. and ed. John Burnaby (Philadelphia: The Westminster Press, 1955), p. 236.

The Discovery of
Human Forgiveness

F orgive us our sins—*that we may discover
our forgiveness of others.*

Thus far I have dealt with human forgiveness as a
problem because of the special nature of relationships
within the family and the powerful reactions stirred by
shame and injury to the self. I have discussed how human
forgiveness is related more to shame than to guilt and how
focusing upon the guilt of another can be used to avoid
one's shame. I also have considered the way in which
forgiveness may become an issue of power and how power,
coupled with rage, is used to defend a person who has been
hurt from further shame and self-injury. Finally, I have
explored how the need to be right or righteous, incorrectly
understood as a Christian virtue, can be substituted for the
pain of not being loved. All of these are significant
dimensions of the problem with human forgiveness, but it is
important now to define and describe some of the ways in
which human forgiveness is commonly understood in order
to clarify further how the understanding of forgiveness
itself can be a problem.

Forgiveness Understood as Attitude and as Act

The most common understanding of human forgiveness
is that it is both attitude and act. *Webster's Third New*

International Dictionary defines *forgiveness* as "an act of forgiving or state of being forgiven." *Forgive* is "to cease to feel resentment against (an offender)" and "to give up claim to requital from or retribution upon" one who has inflicted some injury.[1] Alan Richardson's *Dictionary of Christian Theology* defines *forgiveness* as "the act whereby an injured party allows the party responsible for the injury to go free."[2] Both act and attitude are represented in these definitions. That forgiveness is commonly understood in these ways is what I have repeatedly heard from persons in pastoral counseling.

A useful amplification of the idea of forgiveness as attitude is found in an article published some time ago in *The Philosophical Quarterly.* In contrast to the kind of reasoning which appears in the article, most of us do not deal with interpersonal issues with any awareness of reasoning in a philosophical way. We simply make assumptions without trying to justify them. The assumptions which philosophers examine or try to validate through philosophical analysis are taken for granted by the average person as simply the way things are. R. S. Downie's analysis, therefore, can be a means of clarifying what many of us assume about human forgiveness.

"The concept of forgiveness has been much discussed by theologians," Downie says, "but I shall try to show that an analysis of it can also bring to light points of philosophical interest. The analysis will proceed on the assumption, later defended, that readiness to forgive is a virtue and inability to forgive, or at least unwillingness to try, a vice."[3] The article proceeds by first distinguishing forgiveness from two concepts, "both of which masquerade at times in the guise of forgiveness." They are condonation and pardon. Condoning is saying that a moral offense does not matter when, in fact, it does. Thus, it ignores moral wrong and in effect devalues the persons injured by that wrong. Because condonation is sometimes morally inappropriate, "it cannot be the attitude of forgiveness because readiness to forgive is a virtue, and exercise of a virtue is never morally inappropriate." When we say, "I cannot forgive myself," we mean that we cannot find any excuse for treating our own failure with indulgence and actually mean, I cannot "condone" what has been done.

The concept of pardon, in contrast, involves letting a person off from the merited consequences of his or her actions; "it is to overlook what he has done and to treat him with indulgence." It is condonation with the additional feature of being done by one who is rightfully appointed or formally constituted to condone whatever injury has taken place. Perhaps the most familiar example to Americans was President Ford's pardon of Richard Nixon and the dissatisfaction many persons felt about it. The crucial difference, according to Downie, "between pardoning and forgiving is that we pardon as officials in social roles but forgive as persons." The public official

> sets in motion the normative machinery whereby the offence will be overlooked: he himself need do no more in his official capacity. To say, "I forgive you," however, is not in a similar way to set anything in motion. The forgiver is merely signalling that he has the appropriate attitude and that the person being forgiven can expect the appropriate behaviour.[4]

Forgiving, in contrast to both condonation and pardon, is a personal, not an official, attitude. It is "a loving concern for the dignity of persons viewed as ends in themselves."

> The forgiver is required to prevent any barrier remaining permanently between him and the forgivee (at least on his side for, as we have seen, the forgivee may refuse to accept forgiveness) and to renew trust in him. It is the exhibition of this attitude in action that, together with a belief that injury has been sustained, constitutes forgiveness. It should be noted that the forgiving spirit is not in fact different from the attitude which, it is generally held, should always characterize interpersonal behaviour.

Downie concludes that "the position of forgiveness as a moral good can be justified in terms of secular as well as of religious conceptions." In the secular morality of the West, respect for persons as ends in themselves is the principle in terms of which more specific moral rules and virtues are required to be justified, and "the attitude of *agape* which constitutes the forgiving spirit is the principle of respect for persons in its practical application."[5]

Again, my purpose in presenting the substance of this article is both to clarify the meaning of forgiveness beyond dictionary definition and to suggest that assumptions similar to—if not as conceptually clear as—those discussed here are present in Emmie and Tom. In fact, most of my counselees seem to understand human forgiveness as an appropriate attitude, a virtue, or certainly something a person clearly should have in his or her relationships. And in spite of this belief, persons repeatedly affirm their inability to forgive those in special relations to them.

In addition to common assumptions about human forgiveness as attitude, there are assumptions which treat it primarily as an act. In chapter 3, I noted Hannah Arendt's association of human forgiveness with power, as a faculty which human beings possess and which serves as "the remedy against the irreversibility and unpredictability of the process started by acting." Forgiveness in Arendt's view is an act which can correct, reverse, or release persons from previous actions, thus allowing life to proceed without constant indecision due to fear of consequences. She feels that Jesus' teaching about forgiveness has been neglected in philosophical and political thinking because it has been so closely associated with the Christian religious message. It has, she believes, a more general relevance. She argues that Jesus maintained—against the prevailing religious thought of his day—that "it is not true that only God has the power to forgive, and second that this power does not derive from God . . . but on the contrary must be mobilized by men toward each other before they can hope to be forgiven by God."[6]

In arguing for forgiveness as an essential characteristic of the human condition, Arendt contrasts human "trespasses" and willed evil, concerning herself with the former. The latter, she notes, according to Jesus, "will be taken care of by God in the Last Judgment," which "is not characterized by forgiveness but by just retribution." Trespassing, on the other hand,

> is an everyday occurrence which is in the very nature of action's constant establishment of new relationships within a web of relations, and it needs forgiving, dismissing, in order to make it possible for life to go on by constantly releasing men from what they have done unknowingly.

Only this knowledge that release through forgiveness is constantly available allows us to remain free agents. Freedom through forgiveness allows persons to change their minds and start again, so that they can "be trusted with so great a power as that to begin something new."[7]

She then contrasts forgiveness with vengeance. Vengeance is a reaction against the original trespass which maintains the consequences of the misdeed. In vengeance everyone remains "bound to the process, permitting the chain reaction contained in every action to take its unhindered course." Forgiveness "acts anew and unexpectedly, unconditioned by the act which provoked it and therefore freeing from its consequences both the one who forgives and the one who is forgiven." It is not true, Arendt argues, that "only love can forgive because only love is fully receptive to *who* somebody is." What love is in its narrowly circumscribed sphere, respect is "in the larger domain of human affairs" and respect "is quite sufficient to prompt forgiving of what a person did, for the sake of the person."[8]

It is important to note that the use of Arendt's work both here and in chapter 3 is to illustrate particular points in my argument, the association of forgiveness with power and the widespread assumption that forgiveness is primarily an act. Her major concerns lie elsewhere, in criticizing the consumer totalitarianism of Western society, the reduction of life to the lowest common denominator of "making a living," and the loss of human creativity, the freedom to act and interact meaningfully with others. In order to escape the unreflective routine of life, forgiveness and its consequent allowance of the freedom to correct and change what one has done are necessary. Knowing that forgiveness for trespasses—understood as "missing the mark," not intentional evil—is possible allows humankind to act without undue fear of making mistakes.

The fact that Arendt's dichotomy of trespasses and willed evil is inadequate from a theological perspective to describe the sorts and conditions of human sin does not invalidate the usefulness of her position at this point in our discussion. Arendt's theological judgments are incidental to her main point about forgiveness as a faculty or an act. Moreover, her claim that Jesus' teaching about forgiveness cannot be limited to its religious relevance demonstrates how the concept of forgiveness is employed as practical wisdom about life by persons whose concerns are not at all religious. Her interpretation of Jesus' teaching that the power to forgive "does not derive from God" but "must be mobilized by men toward each other before they can hope to be forgiven by God also" can be understood in the context of her writing as arguing that forgiveness in persons is necessary because it prevents irreversibility and indecisiveness. Understood in the context of the Christian religion, however, it seems to present forgiveness as a manipulative ploy for influencing God or to present humankind as having a great deal of ability to do what is right. Christian theological understanding and my clinical experience suggest the contrary. Arendt's interpretation, however, illustrates how her understanding of Jesus' teaching might be common among both consciously religious persons and those who are essentially unaware of their religious assumptions.

Both Downie and Arendt, presenting their arguments to a secular audience, describe human forgiveness as essential to the framework of Western society. Although my counselees are not philosophers, I believe that most of them come to their struggle with forgiveness with similar assumptions and with at least some conviction that in not forgiving they are not being and doing what they are expected to be and do. Most of them also carry with them some explicit Christian theological assumptions about the necessity of forgiveness to the practice of their faith.

Common Theological Assumptions About Forgiveness

Some of the theological assumptions about human forgiveness carry with them extreme expectations about what forgiving can do if one really does what one ought to do. I make no attempt to survey this literature or to trace its development in Christian history or popular piety. It is sufficient to say that there is a lot of it, and it may appear in almost any publication. One example was shared with me by someone who knew that I was studying human forgiveness. It appeared in *New Woman* magazine, December 1982, and was entitled "A Surprise Law of Healing." I present some of the ideas contained in it not for critique, but simply as an example of a type of literature that influences the assumptions of many persons today.

According to the author, "It is immutable mental and spiritual law that when there is a health problem, there is a forgiveness problem. You must forgive if you want to be permanently healed. . . . Health cannot be accepted by a body that is filled with the poisons generated by unforgiveness." When a person learns how to "think right," according to this author, "you unconsciously relate it to proper rest, diet, exercise and other health habits."

> There is nothing unpleasant or embarrassing about the act of forgiveness. . . . In most instances, you need make no outer contact with those involved in your forgiveness act, unless the occasion arises that demands it. . . . The only requirement is that you willingly speak words of forgiveness, and let those words do their cleansing work. . . . If you have a problem, you have something to forgive. If you experience pain, you have a need to forgive. If you find yourself in unpleasant circumstances, you have a need to forgive. If you find yourself in debt, you have a need to forgive. Where there is suffering, unhappiness, lack, confusion or misery of any sort, there is a need to forgive."[9]

Again, my purpose here is not to evaluate this material in terms of its theological or psychological adequacy, although I think it is seriously inadequate from both perspectives. I am suggesting that material like this has influenced popular assumptions about human forgiveness and that it may come to the public through channels other than those of the traditional religious communions. It often emphasizes the cognitive over the affective and behavioral. Learning "the truth" is all-important, and the truth is often a secret or, in the case of this article, a surprise. The claims about that truth are extreme enough that the reader finds himself or herself thinking, "I'm not sure I believe all of this, but there must be some truth here, and I ought to do something about it." As it appears in the article I have described here, the understanding of forgiveness is strongly associated with the dimension of the Christian tradition that identifies salvation with individual health and that places great emphasis on the beliefs which are necessary for a person who wishes to gain that health. The popular assumption about forgiveness that seems related to articles of this type is that forgiveness is good for you and that you ought to become forgiving as soon as possible.

Biblical interpretation within the mainline religious traditions also contributes to the understanding of forgiveness as something that one ought to do—in this case not so much for one's health as for one's salvation. Although there are a number of passages that touch upon human forgiveness in the Gospels, the one which seems to be most influential, even to those who have little involvement in a particular religious community, is the petition in the Lord's Prayer, "forgive us our trespasses as we forgive those who trespass against us." Dietrich Bonhoeffer in his early writing on the Christian life interprets this petition of the prayer with dogmatic certainty. God will only forgive Christ's followers "if they forgive one another with readiness and brotherly affection."[10] Bonhoeffer wrote this out of a strong sense of Christian community, noting that Christ's followers as a body "bring all their guilt before God and pray as a body for forgiveness." The assumption about what one ought to do, both within and apart from community, that grows out of this interpretation is that we need to forgive others in order to activate God's forgiveness.

William Barclay's *Daily Study Bible,* still popular in

personal religious devotion and in preaching, interprets the same passage as follows:

> Jesus says in the plainest possible language that if we forgive others, God will forgive us; but if we refuse to forgive others, God will refuse to forgive us. . . . If we say, "I will never forget what so-and-so did to me," and then go and take this petition on our lips, we are quite deliberately asking God not to forgive us. . . . No one is fit to pray the Lord's prayer so long as the unforgiving spirit holds sway within his heart.[11]

If Bonhoeffer was dogmatic, Barclay is even more so, and without the context of being primarily a statement about the character of Christian community. The clear implication of Barclay's interpretation is that unless one is worthy through forgiving, one cannot even pray the Lord's Prayer. My point here is not to argue for or against the adequacy of this interpretation of the prayer, but to suggest that it is still a common one and, for the average Bible reader, a natural inference from what the words appear to mean in English. Moreover, the words of the Lord's Prayer are, if not the most familiar words of the Christian tradition, certainly among the most familiar to persons who have had any instruction at all in Christian belief and practice.

Persons like Emmie and Tom, to whom I have referred throughout the book, and a couple like Herman and Hilda, whom I introduced in the last chapter, come to pastoral counseling with assumptions about human forgiveness not unlike those stated in Barclay's interpretation of the Lord's Prayer. They have made statements like, "I just can't forgive him for what he has done," and have suggested by what they say and the way they act that they believe forgiving is something they ought to do, but that they just can't do it. There appears to be something in the relationship with the person who has injured them which prevents them from doing what they think they ought to do. As I understand it, there is a shame they are still dealing with and defending against. In Emmie's case and in Herman's, the defense is righteousness or being right. In Tom's it is holding on to the power that forgiving or not forgiving seems to have. Moreover, at least part of the problem, in my judgment, comes from the church's overconcern with guilt to the neglect of the human problem with shame.

The Church's Involvement in Guilt and Forgiveness

An article by James Lapsley in the late sixties was one of the first influences on my thinking about shame and guilt as it related to the practice of pastoral counseling. In that article, "A Psycho-Theological Appraisal of the New Left,"[12] Lapsley argues that young people "no longer experience guilt and shame the way we did and still do," and that the implications of this "are especially profound for those of us who seek to minister directly to persons."

> Much of our theology, particularly as it gets translated into worship, liturgy, church life, views of the ministry and of pastoral care and counselling, has for long tacitly assumed that it was operating within a guilt culture. . . . Our emphasis upon catharsis, upon the ventilation of hostility and anxiety, the gaining of self-acceptance through the acceptance of the therapist, the emphasis upon insight, all were fundamentally rooted in the confessional model of relationship. . . . One cannot afford, however, to confess much in a shame culture where knowledge of weakness and shortcoming may lead directly to ex-communication.[13]

Although many of Lapsley's descriptions of the way things were in the sixties do not apply to our situation today, the statement about the guilt orientation of worship, liturgy, and church life does seem to me still to be accurate. If ours is not a shame culture, it is certainly one in which we are far more aware of shame, weakness, and inadequacy than when I first began my ministry some thirty years ago. Although the youth culture of the late sixties of which Lapsley wrote has been integrated into and leavened the broader culture of the eighties, the practical or applied theology of the church is still oriented toward guilt.

The discussion of shame and guilt in chapter 2 suggests some of the obvious psychological reasons for this. Guilt is easier to handle. It is related more to specific things done or not done than to the total human condition. It is more related to reason than is shame and thus is more directly accessible to the intervention of others—including the church. With guilt there is more possibility for direct intervention and balancing of punishment with crime than there is with shame. Moreover, if there is any analogous relationship between the function of individuals and that of institutions—and I believe there is—the church and her clergy may be defending themselves against the church's weakness as a force in present-day society through defenses similar to those used by individuals, clinging to its righteousness and its power to forgive sins.

I also noted in chapter 2 the interpretation used by Huber to explain the lack of much previous interest in shame in the Bible—"the general guilt-orientation of Western society." In this judgment she was dependent upon the work of Krister Stendahl, who has challenged the conviction that the apostle Paul can be used to justify a concern for personal guilt. The famous formula, at the same time righteous and sinner, "may have some foundation in the Pauline writings, but this formula cannot be substantiated as the center of Paul's conscious attitude toward his personal sins."[14] Stendahl argues that Paul did not have the type of introspective conscience which such a formula seems to presuppose and that this is likely to be one of the reasons why forgiveness "is the term for salvation which is used least of all in the Pauline writings."

Stendahl's general purpose in the lectures I am examining is "getting behind the hermeneutical to the exegetical level—behind today, behind Luther and Calvin, behind Augustine. . . . We must," he says, "*first* read the Bible to find original meanings and allow those meanings to correct our tendencies to read our own view into the original rather than letting the original stand and speak for itself."[15] Applying this concern to the issue of forgiveness, he notes that in spite of paucity of references to forgiveness in the writings of Paul, "forgiveness is the term most used both in the pulpit and, more generally, in contemporary Western

Christianity to describe the sum total, the fruit, and the effect of the deeds of Jesus Christ."[16]

Stendahl explains this focus upon forgiveness as resulting from the "strong psychological tendency in our minds and interests" and, apparently attempting to induce a little guilt himself, because "we happen to be more interested in ourselves than in God or in the fate of his creation." Christians "outdo the psychologists" in anthropologizing Paul's concerns. Variations of this argument are found in several chapters of his book. He goes back to Augustine to find the beginning of this stream of thought. "His *Confessions* are the first great document in the history of the introspective conscience."

> [It] may well have been that up to the time of Augustine the Church was by and large under the impression that Paul dealt with those issues with which he actually deals: 1) What happens to the Law (the Torah, the actual Law of Moses, not the principle of legalism) when the Messiah has come? 2) What are the ramifications of the Messiah's arrival for the relation between Jews and Gentiles? For Paul had not arrived at his view of the Law by testing and pondering its effect upon his conscience.[17]

The Augustinian monk Martin Luther continued this emphasis upon the guilty conscience in the interpretation of Paul. "Luther's inner struggles presuppose the developed system of Penance and Indulgence, and it is significant that his famous 95 theses take their point of departure from the problem of forgiveness of sins as seen within the framework of Penance." Rudolph Bultmann, in modern times, makes Paul "existential" and affirms "that man is essentially the same through the ages, and that this continuity in the human self-consciousness is the common denominator between the New Testament and any age of human history." "Such an interpretation," says Stendahl, "is an even more drastic translation and an even more far-reaching generalization of the original Pauline material than that found in the Reformers."[18] Stendahl concludes with a strong affirmation that one should be suspicious of a teaching and preaching which pretends that the only door into the church is an "evermore introspective awareness of sin and guilt."

My concern in presenting this material is not to question the importance of sin and guilt as key theological and pastoral issues, but to underscore from a theological as well as a psychological perspective the point made in chapter 2, that emphasis on guilt often results in the neglect of the more powerful, less manipulatable experience of shame. Stendahl's lectures are helpful at another point as well—his examination of Paul's personal concern with "weakness" (*astheneia*) rather than sin. Here, he says, "we find the most experiential level of Paul's theology." In our time, according to Stendahl, extending his previous argument, we tend to equate the two, but this is "a modern misunderstanding."

I believe that this interpretation of weakness in Pauline theology can assist us in putting guilt in proper perspective and taking the experience of shame more seriously. I do not intend to argue that weakness and shame are the same experience or that Paul was afflicted with shame rather than guilt. What I am suggesting is simply that there are some common experiential elements in weakness and shame and that the Pauline understanding of weakness can provide us with a theological means of dealing with the painful experience of shame.

The classic passage, according to Stendahl, where Paul describes his weakness as "a thorn given me in the flesh, messenger of Satan, to harass me" is II Corinthians 12. This weakness was probably a physical illness, sometimes speculated to be epilepsy. At any rate it was a major handicap to Paul, particularly because of the view of the early church "that sickness is really a sign of a lack of that renewing power of life which is the very essence of the Christian existence. A sick apostle is almost like a one-legged football player, a contradiction in terms. . . . The weakness of which Paul speaks is one that comes to him—into him—from without." At no point, says Stendahl, does Paul identify this weakness with sin. On the contrary, it is just one of those things that help him identify himself with the Christ "who was crucified in weakness" (II Cor. 13:4).

Contrary to much popular preaching, Stendahl insists that in II Corinthians 4:7-9 Paul is primarily referring to himself. He, not every Christian, is the one who is "afflicted in every way . . . persecuted . . . struck down." According to Stendahl, "Here is the sick and weak Paul, pitted against the healthy, sun-tanned apostles whom he fights in Corinth. . . . when this rather small, ugly, sick man actually appeared on the scene he seemed not to carry much weight." In the Corinthian correspondence Paul speaks about his weakness in the context of a specific argument about his own authority. "He sees his weakness, his sickness, and the difficulties or shortcomings of his ministry as related to his weakness and as that which teaches him about the nature of Christ's ministry in this world and the nature of Christ's power in this life." Paul says in II Corinthians 11:30, "If I must boast, I will boast of the things that show my weakness." And he proceeds to present himself "the way he wanted the church to know him: unprepossessing, ugly Paul, on the retreat, sneaking out, crumpled in a basket. That is the image of the apostle of Christ . . . which does not allow the glory of God to be overshadowed by cleverness, by achievement, by healthiness."[19]

This seems to me to be a strikingly useful argument for our purposes. Again, I make no attempt to psychologize Paul and present him as a person who experienced shame. I am aware of no evidence for this is his writings. He does, however, appear to be, as Stendahl suggests, a person of "robust conscience, not plagued by introspection." The struggle with limits, with circumstances, with the injury inflicted by others does seem to me to be quite similar to the experience of persons shamed. While Paul's "robust conscience" seems to allow no admission of inadequacy or responsibility for his limitations, persons of less robust conscience might experience a similar situation in terms of inadequacy, impotence, or loss of power. They might feel shame in the perceived scorn of others at their limitations. The importance of Paul in developing a Christian response to our shame is that he managed to identify his weakness with Christ and find power in making that weakness public rather than in vain attempts to hide it. I return to this point later in attempting to relate human and divine forgiveness, but I move now to touch on the work of three pastoral theologians, James Emerson, James Lapsley, and Rodney Hunter, who discuss forgiveness more as something realized than as either an attitude or an act.

The Realization of Forgiveness

Emerson, in his dissertation research, published under the title of *Divorce, the Church, and Remarriage*,[20] made extensive use of the term *realized forgiveness* in order to develop a norm for dealing with the issue of remarriage that seemed more relevant than the legalism of the fifties which attempted to determine the guilty or innocent party in a divorce. In his later book, *The Dynamics of Forgiveness,* he attempted to broaden the application of the concept to the life of the Christian congregation. Realized forgiveness is an experience, not a word. "Just as the basic questions of life are always the same, but the words for expressing those questions change, so with forgiveness: the words that describe 'realized forgiveness' change, but not the experience." The experience of forgiveness, says Emerson, is polar. At one pole is context; at the other, instrumentation. "Forgiveness is a context in which we live"—a context mediated by Jesus Christ. It is to the mediator of the forgiving context that the Christian must be obedient.[21]

At the other pole of the experience of forgiveness is instrumentation, which is "that which gives adequate expression to the context as mediated." Emerson argues with Martin Marty's insistence that forgiveness is not possible apart from law and that "the Law accuses, it does not save."[22] "This," says Emerson, "is wrong. When understood as an instrument by which forgiveness becomes real, precisely the reverse is true. The law is one of the means by which saving forgiveness can come into one's awareness." There is no one means of expressing forgiveness. "No one is bound to old law, to new social custom, or even to a 'vision of the Christlike life.' "[23] It is the Christian fellowship which makes real the context of forgiveness, and Emerson concludes his study by describing the primary purpose of the Christian congregation as implementing the realization of forgiveness in all its activities.

My purpose in presenting this brief summary of Emerson's position is to emphasize forgiveness as something realized rather than something one should do or an attitude one should have. His primary concern is with the experience of God's forgiveness of us rather than our human forgiveness of others. Nevertheless, because of the close connection of human and divine forgiveness in the Christian tradition, if divine forgiveness is something realized in a particular type of context, then it is likely that human forgiveness will be experienced in a similar kind of way. My emphasis later in this chapter on forgiveness as discovery is not unlike Emerson's emphasis on realization. It differs, however, in that the focus of my ministry has been the pastoral counseling center rather than the parish, and I affirm that some of the same experiences of realization of which Emerson speaks can also take place there. Emerson's concern with the law and its place in the realization of forgiveness leads us to the views of Lapsley and Hunter, who focus their attention there.

In an article published in *Theology Today* in 1966, "Reconciliation, Forgiveness, Lost Contracts," James Lapsley affirms the importance of law in the realizing of forgiveness. We continue to use the article in our pastoral care training program because it is one of the few examples of case material being used in a theological journal to make a theological point. In the article, Lapsley argues that "it is not true that the law is dead or dying. Rather, it has gone 'underground' in the experience of most, if not all, persons, and forgiveness is yet a vital necessity in the life of the Christian in the literal sense of release from debt."[24] Over against the emphasis upon reconciliation and minimizing of forgiveness of the Protestant theological giants Barth and Tillich, Lapsley insists that "forgive us our debts as we forgive our debtors" must be taken seriously. Forgiveness presupposes the law. The "question of obligation is inescapable when speaking of forgiveness, and obligation exists only in a legal or quasi-legal framework."[25]

Forgiveness involves the cancellation of "contracts" or obligations between oneself and one's parent surrogates. Although these obligations in most cases exist only in the mind, they are experienced by the person involved as binding contracts to be acted on as such. The attempt to live by these obligations and expecting others to live by them "constitutes one of the primary causes of difficulty in contemporary life." What Lapsley means by "lost contracts" is essentially the same thing that Ivan Nagy means by "invisible loyalties." He uses case material to demonstrate how these hidden obligations appear in a person's life. Although the case involves a number of things, Lapsley intends it to show both the importance of law and experiencing at least the beginning of life transcending the law. He concludes that

> forgiveness is a two step process, involving first the cancellation of "debts" one feels he owes to and is owed by his parents, and second the "forgiveness" of oneself, which becomes possible when reconciliation is experienced as possible. The first of these steps is rather distinct from reconciliation; the second is virtually merged with it. If these distinctions are blurred, something vital is missing and reconciliation becomes an empty phrase, as the underground and its claims remain a barrier between man and God.[26]

One could view the two-step process as dialectical rather than sequential. One can take the first step toward forgiveness when the possibility of reconciliation is felt, but venturing to find one's invisible loyalties or lost contracts may open one both to the need for and possibility of reconciliation. That search may be the needed step of faith without full assurance of success. Whether the relationship is sequential or dialectic, in the light of the function of lost contracts one can see the necessity of both forgiveness and the law in the process of reconciliation.

Like Emerson and Lapsley, another pastoral theologian,

Rodney J. Hunter, also addresses the issues of law, reconciliation, and forgiveness. The message of forgiveness of sins, says Hunter, is "the foundational theme for pastoral care and counseling in the Protestant tradition." Contrasting this theological view to what he perceives to be a dominant theme in certain modern psychologies, Hunter reminds his readers that in the New Testament and in the Reformed faith an understanding of the meaning of freedom is dependent upon an understanding of the law. What has been rejected as moralism in pastoral work was rejected "for inadequate reasons deriving from a misunderstanding of the nature and function of the law in Christian faith. . . . if we deny the possibility of participating in the judging work of God . . . we must similarly deny the possiblity of the appropriateness of proclaiming and embodying the message of divine grace and forgiveness."[27]

> The Good News of the radical love and unmerited forgiveness of God for his people emerged historically through a religious tradition that was through and through moral in its structure, its piety, and its basic sensitivities; and that moral context, with its concern for mutual responsibilities and obligations as expressed in the doctrine of the Law, remains a theologically necessary context for any Christian faith or ministry that seeks to maintain basic continuity with its origins, history, and tradition.[28]

To develop his constructive position, Hunter makes use of Gerhard Ebeling's "Reflections on the Doctrine of the Law" in the book *Word and Faith*. Law, according to Ebeling, is "an event" which is "written in the heart." It is a state of being open to the question of being "accountable in relation and response to someone or something else." The intent of the biblical question "Where art thou?" is, according to Hunter, "Where art thou in relation to me?"—in relation to God, neighbor, and oneself. The work of the law in pastoral care "is nothing fundamentally but the event of calling persons to account for themselves in the multiple relationships, past and present, conscious and unconscious, personal and impersonal, real and fantasied, that constitute human existence as human." When, as pastors, we ask, "What is going on between you and your husband?" or "Where are you now in relation to me?" we are not simply asking out of curiosity. We are calling persons to greater fullness and reality of relationship.

Forgiveness "is unconditional not in the sense that no conditions are in force, but in the sense that the conditions which are in force are nevertheless ultimately not allowed to alienate and destroy the relationship they intended to secure." Interestingly, Hunter's primary example of the kind of pastoral confrontation with the kind of law that he is talking about is a supervisory encounter in CPE when "the discussion turns from the needs and problems of the parishioner to the question of the nature and quality of the student's own involvement in the situation." This, he says, is "one of the distinctive features of CPE, and one of its most profoundly Christian aspects. It witnesses to the claim that the call to responsible living catches us all unprepared, revealing our inward self-deceptions, conflicts, and moral failings. Yet it simultaneously affirms that it is precisely in this recognition that we are most profoundly drawn into community with those whom we serve and with God."[29] Hunter's choice of illustration is interesting in that it raises the question of how often there exists in a Christian congregation the kind of pastoral relationship and the kind of community that would allow such an encounter with the law to take place.

Emerson, Lapsley, and Hunter all affirm the necessity of law in dealing with reconciliation and forgiveness. Emerson sees law as an instrument or means for realizing forgiveness. Lapsley sees the law as having "gone underground" but still having to be dealt with. "Forgive us our debts" refers not primarily to trespasses, the unintended errors of which Arendt speaks, but to real debts and obligations to be resolved. Hunter insists that "the message of forgiveness of sins" is a foundational theme for pastoral care and counseling, but that it has no real meaning apart from law, understood primarily as a calling to accountabilty.

None of the three concerns himself directly with the

problem of human forgiving, but all insist that realizing forgiveness or freedom depends upon relational accountability to self, others, and God. Again, although they do not specifically say this, a relationship which is special or personal requires an accountability based upon something more than right behavior toward another in which one is not at fault. It is an accountability in which one's presence in active communication with the other is more important than what one can claim about his or her behavior. We must assume that human forgiveness would involve the same kind of accountability and that whatever righteousness it produced would be characterized by relation to rather than separation from those persons with whom we have lost contracts and to whom we are accountable.

In the light of these theories of forgiveness and related issues, it seems appropriate to return to some of the persons with whom I have experienced the actual struggle with human forgiveness. How can their situations be understood in terms of the theories which have been presented, and what issues from their lives can enrich our theoretical understanding of this human problem?

Forgiveness in Herman and Hilda, Emmie, and Tom

As the reader may recall, Herman consulted me at the suggestion of his pastor because of his continuing rage toward his wife, Hilda, and his inability to forgive her. I touched on the case material in the previous chapter as an example of self-righteous rage because Herman had told me early in the first interview and continually in subsequent ones of his involvement in church and community activities. Herman was very much aware of the good things he did, and my early interpretation that he was contrasting his goodness to his wife's badness was close enough to his consciousness so as not to be threatening to him. His righteousness, not unlike that of the scribes and Pharisees, was hardly a relational one.

According to Hilda, her affair occurred because she felt out of relationship with Herman. Shortly after the birth of their third child, Herman had told her that he did not love her. As she told of this particular time, some of the power struggle that had been going on between them for a very long time began to emerge. Herman was an accountant who had difficulty handling his own money. He was secretive and irresponsible about his own spending and seemed unable to control his expenditures or be disciplined enough in the jobs he held to make consistent advances and increase his income. Hilda had functioned in the marriage to bail the family out of tight financial scrapes. Finally, in spite of having a very young child she went to work and, perhaps not surprisingly, had had the affair with the employer who had helped to provide some financial and emotional security for her family.

As the marital picture emerged, although Herman's righteousness as a church and community leader remained, in relation to his family he seemed more like a spoiled little boy who depended upon a wife-mother to clean up after him. He had generally been unavailable to help Hilda deal with the effects of the death of her mother just prior to their marriage and with her grief over the recent death of her father. The man she had had her affair with had been the one to do this. The process of pastoral counseling was an attempt to get the emotional needs to which the affair had been an ineffective response into the counseling relationship so that they could be addressed directly.

After several months of seeing them, mostly together, but on occasion separately, it was becoming clearer to both Herman and Hilda that the marital problem was not so much his rage or her affair, but the emotional hunger which both felt and which neither had been able to satisfy in the other. Herman had stopped talking about whether or not he could forgive Hilda for what I would call "shaming" him by the affair. Instead he was talking to me, in her presence, about his seemingly lifelong feelings of inadequacy and never quite measuring up, what it had meant to him to fail the CPA exam, and other failures in his life. Hilda was sharing her grief about having to grow up too quickly and never having anyone upon whom she herself could depend or lean. Quite obviously, both Herman and Hilda were "enjoying" leaning on me. They were using pastoral counseling—using me—to satisfy some basic human needs which they had denied they had.

I emphasize what was going on apart from the issue of forgiving or not forgiving in order to point to the conditions under which forgiveness can be discovered. In the midst of an experience in which basic human needs are being satisfied, not secretly, but openly, a person can give up some of the complaints about those who supposedly have denied his or her needs. Herman and Hilda reported that at home they were talking more directly and openly to each other. The communication was not always happy, but it seemed honest, and consequently, each expressed more trust in and respect for the other.

During one of our times together, Hilda reported an incident in Sunday school when she was asked to read the Ten Commandments.

Hilda:	I knew I was going to get to the seventh, and I did. The strange thing about it—and nobody there knew what was going on inside me—I knew for the first time that I was talking about myself. I was one who had committed adultery. I didn't think about all the reasons that justified my doing it. I knew I had wronged myself as well as Herman.
Pastor:	It sounds like you knew what it felt like to be a sinner instead of just knowing it in your head.
Hilda:	I think so. And I felt better feeling it, if that makes any sense, like I had been looking outside myself at what was wrong with Herman for too long.
Pastor:	(to Herman) Did you know what was happening with Hilda?
Herman:	She told me about it later on. I was glad she felt that.
Pastor:	It relieved you of the responsibility of having to remind her.
Herman:	The main difference for me is not being so angry. I think about what's wrong with me more than what's wrong with Hilda.
Pastor:	I'm glad you can let yourself think about that. It sounds like you're seeing that you're both a lot alike.
Herman:	I hadn't thought about that much until recently. We've been through a lot together. I don't feel happy

> about the things that have happened, but I do feel a lot more peaceful.

Pastor: I suspect that you may have forgiven her without being aware of it. At least your commitment to going on sounds like that to me. In spite of what you have done to each other, you're going on.

Herman: I think so. I remember that scripture in the Sermon on the Mount about seeing the speck in somebody else's eye and not seeing the log in my own.

Pastor: Yeah, I think what we've been doing is getting so we could talk about the logs instead of the specks.

Now let me say immediately that this dialogue is neater than most of them. The hundred or so situations that I have shared with persons for whom the issue of human forgiveness seemed in some way to work out seldom had this kind of discovery become obvious in one particular session. I made note on this one and on the sessions with Emmie and Tom because they were unusual. Moreover, the "verbatims" were constructed from notes made after the session, not from a tape recording. I am sure that there are distortions in them as well as the changes I made in order to respect the privacy of Herman and Hilda and the other persons whose stories are presented. What I am convinced of, however, is that what seems to me to be the essential message of this pastoral encounter consistently appears in all the situations of human forgiveness in which I have participated. Forgiveness is a discovery after the fact, not something sought after and achieved by whatever religious or psychological means.

Emmie "forgave" Elmer after discovering her feelings for a married man whom she had met at her place of employment. I use quotation marks to point out that I believe she discovered forgiveness without ever using the word. She maintained her judgment that what Elmer had done was wrong and that, even though tempted, she had not succumbed to the same temptation. She was aware, however, that she was tempted even as he was. Emmie had difficulty talking about this with me, but our relationship was long enough and personal enough that we could often point to what was going on without using the words. She was able to write Elmer and deal with his not paying alimony in a way that was more realistic than vindictive, and the words of the letter as she read them to me indicated an acceptance of him that I had never heard from her before.

The question remains in Emmie's case as to the power of words of forgiveness or interpretations about the meaning of forgiveness. As I reflect upon Emmie's situation several years after the experience I can imagine the usefulness of my interpreting some of my understanding of human forgiveness to her. As the situation actually occurred, I simply suggested to her on several occasions that her attitude toward Elmer appeared to have changed. As I presented the interaction in chapter 1, I commented:

Pastor: Elmer sounds almost human!

Emmie: What?

Pastor: I never had thought of him as an ordinary human being before, but listening to you then, the thought did occur to me. You sounded as if you were concerned about his predicament.

Emmie: Well, he got himself into it.

Pastor: I know. I was just noticing how you sounded. For the first time I can remember, he didn't sound like the enemy—just an ordinary human being. [I sighed and commented that it felt good. Emmie remained silent.]

Perhaps the reader will wonder about what appears to be sarcasm in my response to Emmie, and perhaps I need again to say that my being able to be sarcastic grows out of a long-term relationship and the fact that I had great respect and affection for this woman. My use of this kind of indirection was an attempt to get around her resistance to doing what people had been telling her to do for years: "Forgive Elmer—and get along with the business of your life." A positive response to that suggestion—however useful it might appear as a general rule—would have placed her in the position she had occupied virtually all of her life, doing what people said she ought to do or what would be good for her.

My concern had been to try to mobilize more of the power

of her rage toward Elmer as a positive force in her life. Her anger toward him was a problem primarily because she had to convince herself of her righteousness in order to justify it. Her rage, however, had not only gotten in her way, it had enlivened her life, and that was what I was trying to help her value and keep as a resource for living. An angry response to me and my sarcasm might, in the context of a long, caring relationship, allow her to put me in my place yet at the same time maintain her own place in relation to me. If the theological implication of this can be generalized beyond Emmie's situation—and I believe it can—to tell persons to forgive is to proclaim salvation by good works. To help them discover that they have forgiven is to acquaint or reacquaint them with a power already operating in their lives. Whether that power is named or not seems less important than its discovery.

This is not to say that words of forgiveness are not important. They are, and when it seems appropriate to use the words, I believe in using them. In Emmie's case, however, experiencing the reality of her accepting Elmer as a person not completely different from herself seemed like what was possible at the time. Had I insisted on telling her that she had forgiven Elmer, I believe that she would have resisted this as inconsistent with her sense of judgment and his accountability for what he had done. There were many things left to be worked through, and had she continued on in counseling with me, I believe that they would have been. Her feelings of caring for me, however, were so intense that they seemed inconsistent with her feelings about the new person in her life. And Emmie was not one who could easily handle contradictions.

Most of us who are involved in trying to facilitate healing need to let Emmie speak to us, for her problem with human forgiveness has much theological wisdom in it. As Downie helpfully distinguished, there is a significant difference between forgiveness and condonation. Genuine forgiveness does not come cheaply. I feel fortunate that people like Emmie have helped me avoid obscuring that fact with my concern for a quicker cure.

The dialogue with Tom is an example of a more explicit discussion about human forgiveness, but there is sarcasm and indirection in it as well. Part of Tom's problem was the way in which he dealt with authority. Telling him what he ought to do—forgive his father and accept him like another human being—would have simply been continuing an old pattern, whether or not he chose to do or not to do what I told him. My intent in the dialogue was to facilitate the discovery of his father's humanness and Tom's likeness to him without simply telling him that was the way things were. Actually, I could not *know* that anyway. I could only surmise, so I responded to Tom's feelings about his father's sharing some of his own fallibility and weakness.

Pastor:	What's the lump? Discovering that he had problems too?
Tom:	Wondering if I really can forgive him.
Pastor:	It's hard to give up that power.
Tom:	Power?
Pastor:	You sound more like a priest than a son. Go back to the lump in your throat.
Tom:	What do you mean?
Pastor:	I felt more forgiveness when you told me about the lump than when you began to speculate on whether you could forgive him or not.
Tom:	It did seem more real—but scary.
Pastor:	Coming down from the seat of power is scary. If your dad is human like you, you might find you can have something more with him than some occasional time together.

Although the dialogue explicitly involves forgiveness, my effort is, obviously, to stay close to the affective dimension of Tom's relationship to his father and to me rather than to discuss my theories about forgiveness. Actually, I had an unusual opportunity to carry out the theory in practice, rather than talk *about* it. In the internal debate about whether he can forgive or not, Tom is concentrating more on his position or role in relation to his father rather than allowing his feelings about him to speak. When the discussion about the girlfriend develops, another opportunity arises—this time to get at the common humanity which Tom and his father share.

Pastor: It sounds like you're ashamed of her.

Tom: Yeah. It feels like that.

Pastor: You chose to confront your dad about the importance of bringing Betty, and now it doesn't seem that you have much to show off to them. She's acting weak and dependent upon you.

Tom: I wish it were the way it was when I first met her. Now I'm feeling trapped.

Pastor: Oh! (*expressing some surprise*) Then your father's not the only one in the family who's had to suffer with an inadequate woman. (*pause*) But, of course, you would never be disloyal like he was.

Tom: What do you mean?

Pastor: I was just thinking about how it seemed like your dad left your mother because he felt there was something wrong with her, and how you thought you needed to be better than that.

Tom: (*after some silence*) That feels like it may be it.

Pastor: You may be like the old son-of-a-gun in spite of yourself.

Tom: (*silence*)

Pastor: (*responding to Tom's sad look*) What's your sadness about?

Tom: I don't know. I guess I'm ashamed of being that little and self-centered. I ought to care more for Betty now, but I don't want to.

Pastor: I guess it runs in the family.

Tom: Damn you!

The remainder of the dialogue involved an interpretation about Tom's grandiosity having been punctured and a sharing with him of that classic phrase from the Elijah story, "I am no better than my fathers." Whether Tom picked up on that or not is not clear. At that point I may have been more fascinated with my own ideas than staying with Tom. My theory was that the myth of besting the father was being acted out, whether the source of the myth was biblical, oedipal, or whatever. Fortunately, any digression on my part did not seem to get in Tom's way. Our relationship was such that I did not distract him, and he moved back to his resonance with his father's pain and his identification with him. He responded to me, but not dutifully following the course he might have perceived I wanted for him. Rather, he moved by his own choice to identify with his real father and share a common humanity with him.

As is no doubt obvious by now, I believe that it is in the discovery of likeness to the father, rather than in talking about forgiving him, that genuine forgiveness lies. Most of my efforts in the interaction were directed toward facilitating that discovery. Again, as in Emmie's situation, the dialogue does not stand by itself. It takes place in a relationship where both affection and anger had appeared before. I was free to push and poke at Tom because he had experienced my caring about him and the stories of his pilgrimage. He knew that I respected both his father and his anger toward his father.

I see this incident as one in which forgiveness is discovered. It is one in which I might have said, "I think you have forgiven your father," but, quite frankly, that might have been said more for my satisfaction than for Tom's. More important was the discovery, not my interpretation of it—at least not at that time. More important was the relationship which created conditions under which this and other discoveries could take place.

In this chapter, I have explored the problem with human forgiveness as it has appeared in the concept of forgiveness itself. The understanding of forgiveness as attitude and as act are both problematic in that they contribute to the view that forgiveness is something that we should try hard to do or to have. I have presented examples of the abundance of literature which suggests that our forgiving is necessary both for our own health and for God's forgiveness. It appears, on the one hand, that forgiveness has been central enough to the church's understanding of itself that the works righteousness inherent in these views has been insufficiently addressed. On the other hand, if the problem of works righteousness has been addressed, it has often been done by emphasizing the reconciling work of God and not dealing with human forgiveness at all.

Pastoral theologians Emerson, Lapsley, and Hunter have each addressed that part of the problem and have insisted that it is not sufficient to deal with God's work alone. The human dimension, the process of realizing forgiveness, the lost contracts, the calling to accountability represented by the law must be taken into account. What I have done, in suggesting through my clinical material that human forgiveness is not primarily either attitude or act but discovery, is to unfold another part of the problem's human dimension, one that it is essential for pastoral work. And, as usual, while this helps to answer some questions, it raises others. The most obvious one is, How does one seek to discover something without the discovery simply becoming another work to be achieved? How do pastors facilitate this in their caring for persons? In what way can what happened to Herman and Hilda, Emmie, and Tom be typical or normative for others to whom we minister? These are a few of the practical but difficult questions which must be addressed. Necessary to answer them, however, is the final element in the problem with human forgiveness: the way human and divine forgiveness are related.

Notes

1. *Webster's Third New International Dictionary* (Springfield, Mass.: G. & C. Merriam Co., 1976), p. 891.

2. Alan Richardson, ed., *A Dictionary of Christian Theology* (Philadelphia: The Westminster Press, 1969), p. 130.

3. R. S. Downie, "Forgiveness," *The Philosophical Quarterly* 15 (April 1965):128.

4. Ibid., p. 132.

5. Ibid., pp. 133-34.

6. Arendt, *Human Condition*, p. 239.

7. Ibid., p. 240.

8. Ibid., p. 243.

9. Catherine Ponder, "A Surprise Law of Healing," *New Woman* (December 1982), pp.70-72, excerpted from *The Dynamic Laws of Healing*, copyright 1966 by Catherine Ponder.

10. Dietrich Bonhoeffer, *The Cost of Discipleship* (London: SCM Press, 1959), pp. 149-50.

11. William Barclay, *The Gospel of Matthew* I (Philadelphia: The Westminster Press, 1959): 223-24.

12. James N. Lapsley, "A Psycho-Theological Appraisal of the New Left," *Theology Today* 25, no. 4 (January 1969): 446-61.

13. Ibid., p. 460.

14. Krister Stendahl, *Paul Among Jews and Gentiles* (Philadelphia: Fortress Press, 1976), p. 82.

15. Ibid., p. 36.

16. Ibid., p. 24.

17. Ibid., p. 84.

18. Ibid., p. 88.

19. Ibid., pp. 40-42, 46-47, 50.

20. James G. Emerson, *Divorce, the Church, and Remarriage* (Philadelphia: The Westminster Press, 1961).

21. James G. Emerson, *The Dynamics of Forgiveness* (Philadelphia: The Westminster Press, 1964), pp. 163-64.

22. Martin E. Marty, *The Hidden Discipline* (St. Louis: Concordia Publishing House, 1962), p. 32.

23. Emerson, *Dynamics*, pp. 99-100.

24. James N. Lapsley, "Reconciliation, Forgiveness, Lost Contracts," *Theology Today* 23, no. 1 (April 1966):45-46.

25. It is interesting to note the difference in this point of view from Arendt's understanding of the "trespass" as an unintentional injury resulting from human action. I am not concerned with deciding which is the more adequate interpretation. From the point of view of the author's primary concern, each of them is useful. Moreover, the obligation may exist whether the injury was intentional or not.

26. Lapsley, "Lost Contracts," pp. 58-59.

27. Rodney J. Hunter, "Law and Gospel in Pastoral Care," *The Journal of Pastoral Care* 30, no. 3 (September 1976): 146, 147, 151.

28. Ibid., p. 152.

29. Ibid., p. 156.

Humanity Forgiven
and Forgiving

F orgive us our sins—*as we are reminded*
of our relationship to you and to those with
whom relationship has been most difficult.

I have thus far presented human forgiveness as a
personal and pastoral problem which has not sufficiently
been acknowledged as such—as a kind of Christian family
myth that is revered and assumed to be a certain way but is
not adequately open to inspection in the light of the actual
relationships between persons. One dimension of the
problem has been the special character of relationships
between parents and children and between husbands and
wives which significantly affects the way in which ethical
principles apply to them.

Human forgiveness has been a problem also because
forgiveness has been associated with the more manageable
factor of guilt, whereas human forgiveness—particularly
between those in special relations with each other—involves
the more irrational experience of shame. Shame cannot be
addressed simply through specific actions or attitudes, but
must be dealt with in terms of a response to the life of the
whole person, not just to what has been done. Human
forgiveness has been a problem also because of the defenses
which persons use against shame: rage, power, and

[147]

righteousness. In the previous chapter, I looked at some of the common assumptions about human forgiveness itself and some of the important additional problems that must be dealt with in presenting a theory of human forgiveness that is basically continuous with the Christian tradition and also takes seriously the problems which have been identified. I began to develop some of the clues which seem evident in clinical material from pastoral counseling into a point of view that human forgiveness is more a *discovery* than the traditional understanding of it as attitude or act. What I attempt to do here is to extend this understanding of forgiveness by relating it to some of the major elements of the Christian tradition with regard to forgiveness.

Because of its importance in the church's understanding of the Christian life, human forgiveness seems to me to have been revered beyond adequate examination and criticism. The kind of criticism that has appeared has often come indirectly through affirming the power of God's reconciling action—in effect making forgiveness relatively unimportant. I understand forgiveness between persons to be an important and essential part of God's reconciliation of us with each other. It functions, however, more as a witness that God's reconciliation has taken effect than as something we are required to do in conformity to an external standard. This is not the only view of human forgiveness that appears in the New Testament, but it is a view which is consistent with the central thrust of Jesus' teaching, and it can offer a valuable interpretive framework for the pastor in the work of pastoral care and counseling.

More specifically, what I attempt to argue through the examination of the biblical and theological materials in this chapter is that forgiveness is discovered not in trying to forgive or in being instructed about the process of forgiveness, but in the larger process of reconciliation which is concretely expressed in human life through overcoming one's shame and rediscovering who one is beyond the experience of injury and brokenness. The person who concentrates upon whether he or she can forgive is not likely to do so. The human quest is for a larger, more important goal: what Barth calls "fellowmanhood" or what I have found useful to call "relational humanness" or "neighbor-hood." The issue of human forgiveness needs to be put into perspective just as it is in the Lord's Prayer—we forgive our debtors as a part of all the petitions of the prayer: in recognizing our relationship to God and his kingdom, in his gift of the days of our lives, in his forgiveness of our sins, and in the recognition of his presence in the temptations and evil of the life we face as his children. Such a quest is large enough to deal with our shame and our tendencies to use power and righteousness to defend against it.

I move now to examine how biblical materials having to do with human forgiveness have been interpreted by New Testament scholars. Because my competence lies elsewhere, I am doing this "secondhand" through the work of other interpreters. I make no attempt to survey all of the relevant material. I hope simply to demonstrate that the point of view I have come to, primarily out of the experience of persons struggling with forgiveness in their lives, is not inconsistent with competent New Testament scholarship. In fact, I believe it adds an integrative perspective that brings out the relevance of some of these New Testament studies to persons today without distorting what seems to be the text's original meaning. Sufficient consciousness of the difference between the present and biblical times can allow the ancient text to be used in a modern context without an inappropriate distortion of its meaning.

The major resource for developing a New Testament view of human forgiveness is the teaching of Jesus. As I suggested in the previous chapter, following Stendahl, forgiveness was not an important concern in the writings of Paul. In my examination of Jesus' teaching, the major focus is upon the Lord's Prayer as it appears in Matthew and Luke because the petition of the prayer which has to do with our forgiving our debtors is both the most familiar and the most troublesome to persons who have been injured by others. This concern is not inconsistent with that of the scholars who are primarily involved in interpreting the teachings of

Jesus because the prayer has been judged to be among the most authentic of Jesus' sayings. "Intensive work on the material in the synoptic gospels shows that there are four aspects of that material where we can come close to the words of the historical Jesus. These are the proclamation of the Kingdom of God, the proverbial sayings, the parables, and the Lord's Prayer."[1] In order to develop an adequate understanding of human forgiveness in the Lord's Prayer, however, it is important to give attention to other teachings of Jesus on forgiveness and, most important, to do this in the context of an interpretation of Jesus' teaching about the kingdom of God.

The Kingdom as a Context for Human Forgiveness

Although using a text out of its specific context may not be a credible way for a pastoral theologian to begin a section on biblical interpretation, the assurance given in Matthew 6:33—that seeking first God's kingdom and righteousness will put all other issues in proper perspective—seems to me to put Jesus' teaching on human forgiveness in the proper relationship to his total message. The announcement of the kingdom is at the forefront of all that Jesus taught, just as the petition about the kingdom appears before the petition about forgiveness in the Lord's Prayer.

"There is no doubt that the proclamation of the Kingdom of God is the central aspect of the message of Jesus. But having said that, one has to ask what it means to say that Jesus proclaimed the Kingdom of God." In answering that question, Norman Perrin concludes that Jesus' message of the kingdom has a double focus. "On the one hand, there is certainly a future aspect to the Kingdom in his message; on the other hand, there is equally certainly a reference to present experience of the Kingdom, to the mediation of existential reality in the present."[2]

With respect to the kingdom's future aspect, Jesus' teaching presents a final state of the redeemed where God's kingly activity will be clearly expressed for all to see. As the Beatitudes suggest, it is a state in which the values of the world are reversed and the values of God established. The poor become rich. Mourners are comforted. The meek inherit the earth. To me the most powerful and persuasive picture of this state in the New Testament is the messianic banquet described in Matthew 8:11: "I tell you, many will come from east and west and sit at the table with Abraham, Isaac, and Jacob in the kingdom of heaven." The metaphor of eating and drinking together seems most adequately to symbolize "the sharing of the eternal blessings of God."[3]

In the central kingdom image of table fellowship, there is a reversal of the expected sharing of blessings. Those "from the east and west" included the "tax collectors and sinners." Something of the relationship between the kingdom in the present and in the future can be seen in the common life of Jesus and his followers, where "scribe, tax collector, fisherman and Zealot came together around the table at which they celebrated the joy of the present experience and anticipated its consummation in the future."[4] This is the same kind of reversal which the Beatitudes describe; the guests at the family table are unexpected ones. At the banquet of the kingdom, God only knows beside whom we may sit or, for that matter, if the guests we expected will be there at all.

With respect to its present aspect, the familiar phrase, "the kingdom of God is in the midst of you" is most expressive of Jesus' teaching. In contrast to what is expected of him by those who compared him to other leaders, Jesus refused to speak of signs of the kingdom. Signs are associated with history as it is usually understood—with kings, wars, and events to be observed "out there." The kingdom, as it is experienced now, is in the midst of ordinary and unexpectedly important people, those who hear and see that God's rule is in fact a part of their lives.

Perrin's later work is strongly influenced by a literary critical approach to the parables and proverbial sayings of Jesus. From that perspective he views the kingdom of God as what Philip Wheelwright has identified as a "tensive symbol"—one which "can have a set of meanings that can neither be exhausted nor adequately expressed by any one referent."[5] In the Lord's Prayer, for example, once it is recognized that the kingdom of God is being used as a tensive symbol in the opening petition, the remaining petitions become particularly interesting; they represent realistic possibilities for the personal or communal experience of God as king.

> God is to be experienced as king in the provision of "daily bread," in the experienced reality of the forgiveness of sins, and in support in the face of "temptation." Is is very evident that the symbol Kingdom of God evokes the expectation of the activity of God on behalf of the petitioner, and that the symbol is by no means exhausted in any one manifestation of that which it evokes.[6]

The kingdom of God is a narrative means of demonstrating "the inner meaning of the universe and of human life," not a "single identifiable event which every man experiences at the same time," but something "which every man experiences in his own time."[7]

I am neither concerned with nor capable of arguing for the adequacy of Perrin's view of the kingdom among other views. It does seem to me, however, to underscore the evocative power of the symbol in both its present and its future dimension: God's kingly activity going on even now in the midst of the ordinary events of life and, finally, God's blessings provided in an unpredictable, unexplainable way to just those persons whom we might have turned away from his banquet. Those two images of the kingdom, each suggesting surprise (my emphasis, not necessarily Perrin's), provide the context for looking at Jesus' specific teaching about human forgiveness, first outside the Lord's Prayer and then within it.

How Often Shall I Forgive My Brother?

"One of the distinctive elements in the teaching of Jesus is his stress on the forgiveness of the brother. In the new age forgiveness of sin is conditional not only upon repentance and faith, but also upon forgiveness of others."[8] Although the conditional nature of forgiveness seems to me to be highly questionable, the association of forgiveness of the brother with the meaning of the kingdom of God does seem to be central to Jesus' teaching. The saying about forgiving one's brother is found both in Matthew and Luke. In Matthew it appears immediately prior to the parable of the unmerciful servant as a kind of introductory teaching on forgiveness. The point of the parable, however, appears to have nothing to do with the number of times a person should forgive. Its message is more general, namely, that the kingdom of God is known in terms of God's forgiveness of sins and that the only proper response to that experience is our own forgiving. The human task is to imitate God's action for us in our relationship to other persons.[9]

In the discussion of how often the brother should be forgiven, Matthew seems to be involved in developing a rule for church discipline. Forgiving is to be practiced, not so much as a style of life but according to rules which, in fact, give one political power in relation to others. As Matthew 18:18-19 puts it, "Whatever you bind on earth will be bound in heaven, and whatever you loose on earth will be loosed in heaven. . . . if two of you agree on earth about anything they ask, it will be done for them by my Father in heaven." (Recall the discussion of power as a defense in chapter 3.) Whatever else it may be, this passage appears to be both an elaboration and a distortion of Jesus' central message about forgiveness.

That central message as it appears in both Matthew and Luke emphasizes the exaggerated or uncharacteristic nature of human forgiveness. Moreover, as C. F. D. Moule emphasizes, "the controlling factor cannot be anything so abstract and impersonal as justice," The "costliness of forgiveness" is rooted in the "preciousness of persons," not principles.[10] Whatever the details about the quantity of forgiveness, it was far more than what was natural or expected. The emphasis upon number is meant to express Jesus' teaching that in the light of the kingdom, human forgiveness occurs unexpectedly and to an unexpected degree, not to emphasize how many times it should occur.

Peter's question and Jesus' answer temper and modify the structure of church discipline and the power element in the offering of forgiveness since (1) Peter, the premiere church leader, is specifically mentioned; (2) the "brother" (cf. 18:15) is to be forgiven a *limitless* number of times; and (3) no requirement of confession or repentance is mentioned in 18:21-22.

In the parable of the unmerciful servant, the servant initially freed from indebtedness to his master has not really "discovered" forgiveness. He is not yet able to see himself in the same plight as the second servant who owes him money. In reflecting upon this portion of scripture, David Norris, in his dissertation study of forgiving, has suggested that a person who expresses forgiveness in the way revealed in the parable can do so only through participating "in a kind of healing so profound, so deeply connected to the core of reality, that even the concept of 'sin against me' has little meaning. Instead of responding with anger and rejection, such a person would respond with humility and with a recognition of the other person's woundedness."[11] Also relevant to understanding the forgiving of the brother is the picture of the last judgment in Matthew 25:37-40, in which the "righteous" are unaware of their specific acts of ministry to others.

Describing who "the brother" is in Jesus' teaching is, however, most effectively done in the parable of the good Samaritan. The Samaritan or brother is probably the person to whom it is most difficult for us to respond, although I cannot claim that this is the original meaning of the parable. This interpretation, however, seems to me to be in keeping with the vision of the messianic banquet and its surprising dinner guests. Most often these guests are understood to be the outcasts of society, and undoubtedly in the light of Jesus' message and ministry they are. It is difficult to believe, however, that the parable is intended to have only a message for society and not for interpersonal relationships as well. If the latter is the case, the Samaritan may indeed be a person with whom we have a special but estranged relationship—a parent, a child, or a spouse. It does not seem inappropriate to suggest that Jesus' vision of neighbor-hood may have included depth as well as breadth of relationship.

Human Forgiveness in the Lord's Prayer

Because the Lord's Prayer is the most familiar piece of Christian literature, it has been most influential in forming popular religious beliefs about human forgiveness. In the previous chapter I pointed to one of the most common and troublesome of these beliefs—that forgiveness is something we ought to do and that God's forgiveness of us is conditional upon our doing it. It seems clear that such an understanding of human forgiveness does appear in the New Testament. An examination of some of the recent interpretation of the Lord's Prayer by New Testament scholars, however, can reveal the origin of this interpretation of the prayer's meaing and help us move toward a view which is more consistent with the central thrust of the Christian message.

I begin by examining the prayer as a whole. Many religious difficulties arise from isolating particular texts and making behavioral inferences from their apparent meaning apart from the context in which the text appears. Viewing the prayer as a whole—and here I continue to be more dependent upon Perrin and his teacher Jeremias than on any other source—the most striking and perhaps most important thing about it is the fact that Jesus taught his disciples to address God as *Abba.* Jeremias points out that Jewish prayers

> do not contain a single example of *abba* as an address for God; Jesus on the other hand always used it when he prayed (with the exception of the cry from the cross). . . . It was something new, something unique and unheard of, that Jesus dared to take this step and to speak with God as a child speaks with his father, simply, intimately, securely.[12]

"It is only against this background," says Jeremias, "that we can understand the deepest meaning of the Lord's

Prayer."[13] The disciples are taught to use the child's word for God, in spite of the fact that such a practice was specifically forbidden in all that they had been previously taught about religious practice. "The same point," Perrin notes, "is made negatively in the saying recorded as Mark 10:15 par.: 'Whoever does not *receive* the Kingdom of God like a child shall not enter it.' " He notes that the saying in Mark probably has a future reference and that the *Abba* of the Lord's Prayer is a present one, but that this is simply an indication of the ever-present tension between present and future in the teaching of Jesus. The "manifestation of the kingly activity of God in history and human experience is to lead to this new relationship with God. This is to be enjoyed now (*abba*) and it will in some way be consummated in the future (Mark 10:15 par.)."[14]

Perrin sees this tension between present experience and future consummation throughout the prayer. Another scholar, Raymond Brown, who like Perrin emphasizes the unity of the prayer, sees the focus upon the future as the overriding dimension of the prayer. The term *eschatological* as Brown uses it refers to the end time symbolized by the messianic banquet. This eschatological viewpoint of the prayer, he says, "binds together the petitions into one picture," but in Luke's rendering of the prayer, "the intensity of eschatological aspiration has begun to yield to the hard facts of daily Christian living. . . . Give us each day our daily bread" (Luke 11:3). Brown seems disappointed with this everyday practicality and concludes his essay with the recommendation, "As we say the prayer nineteen centuries later, now completely enmeshed in the temporal aspect of the Christian life, it would, perhaps, profit us to revive in part some of its original eschatological yearning."[15]

If we accept the unity of the prayer in the light of the new, childlike relationship to the God whom we call *Abba*, if we accept the prayer's concern for both the kingdom now and the kingdom to come, what is the meaning of the teaching about human forgiveness in the fifth petition? According to Perrin, the parts of the prayer which are most dissimilar from Jewish prayers of the period and, as such, authentic emphases of Jesus' teaching are the address *Abba* and the phrase from Luke 11:4, "as we ourselves forgive every one who is indebted to us." We might reasonably conclude, then, that as a prayer which is expressive of the kingdom, partly experienced now and fully experienced in the future, these distinctive elements seem to be affirming that God's relationship to us expresses forgiveness and that as children of God, our relationships to others are also forgiving ones.

The problem with human forgiveness, as it grows out of interpretation or misinterpretation of the Lord's Prayer, is that a condition of the kingdom—meaning an affirmation of what the kingdom is like only partially now but fully in God's time—seems to have been quickly made into a condition *for entering* the kingdom. This element in the teaching of Jesus seems to have been picked up by the Gospel writers as instruction for new converts[16] and interpreted conditionally (Matt. 6:14 and Mark 11:25) that God will forgive us *if* we forgive others (italics and interpretation of this particular point mine). And it is this interpretation of the petition that has been changed from an affirmation of the way things are and shall be to a part of present-day assumptions about what one, as a Christian, should do.

Perrin's work on this passage seems to me to support the kind of interpretation that I have made. He does not make the "conditional element" in the prayer sequential, i.e., God forgiving us because we have first forgiven others, but he links them inseparably together as an illustration of the way that eschatology and ethics are linked. He quotes appreciatively Jeremias's phrase, "the willingness to forgive is the outstretched hand, by which we grasp God's forgiveness," which suggests that God's forgiveness and ours may be simultaneous. Jesus is concerned above all, says Perrin, "with the experience of the individual who responds to the challenge of the kingly activity of God" and is, therefore, "caught up in the eschatological tension between present and future." The forgiving relationship to others is the kind of response which must be made to the proclamation of the kingdom "in order that man may enter even more fully into that which is offered to him as God manifests himself as King in the ministry of Jesus."[17]

Raymond Brown avoids the conditional by emphasizing the eschatological to the exclusion of the "kingdom now" dimension. When the petition is properly understood, he says, "there is no *quid pro quo,* nor is there a question of the priority of human forgiveness." As in I John 4:20, "He who does not love his brother whom he has seen, cannot love God whom he has not seen." "In the last days the followers of Christ will receive the fullness of divine sonship. Their forgiveness of one another as brothers and their forgiveness by their Father are both parts of this great gift."[18]

Another interpretation, published in German more than forty years ago and written some time before that, is that of Ernst Lohmeyer. Lohmeyer's contribution, as I compare it to other discussions of the forgiveness petition of the prayer, comes at the point of interpreting the concept of debt. "Debts," he says, "are no individual details of man's life, but man in his totality before God." He contrasts the legal and religious meaning of debt and notes that legally a debt can be paid off and the relationship resolved. With respect to the obligation between God and humankind, however, our indebtedness is so great that it can never be exactly calculated and paid off. The "relationship between God and man is a personal one, not bound by a rigid necessity. . . . It is the free and immediate will of the king that frees the servant from his tremendous debt with a word; it is the father who restores his lost son with a kiss on the cheek."[19]

The text of the prayer suggests that there is a parallel between our forgiveness and God's. Lohmeyer insists, however, that theologically this cannot be and that in fact there is a complete difference between them. Other persons are simply not indebted to us in the manner and degree to which we are indebted to God; therefore, "the equality on the one hand and the difference on the other force us to the conclusion that our 'human forgiveness' can and must be understood simply as a reflection of the divine forgiveness."[20]

[158]

Lohmeyer's interpretation is an interesting example of resolving a problem in the scriptural text with a theological interpretation drawn from outside that text. The problem of the text's apparent suggestion that God's forgiveness of us is conditioned by our forgiveness of others is ruled out by a theological judgment based upon a more general understanding of humankind's relation to God which precludes this. Friedrich Hauck, in his article on the word *debt* in Kittel's *Theological Wordbook of the New Testament,* comments in a footnote that the thought "that God has given man everything, and that man owes all that he is and has to God is wrongly imported into the context by Lohmeyer."[21] On the same point, Norris comments that "although Lohmeyer's theological analysis of the human condition is correct, its application to this petition is not."[22] I would simply suggest, from the point of view of an observer of New Testament scholarship, that although I also agree with Lohmeyer's theological point about human dependency and believe that theological interpretation based upon issues outside of immediate textual considerations is not only inevitable but necessary, Lohmeyer seems to resolve the problem too easily by saying that human forgiveness is merely a reflection of the divine. In doing so, he undercuts the affirmation of responsibility for one's neighbor that is so strongly present throughout Jesus' teachings.

In the light of that vision of life, the kingdom as neighbor-hood, it is also difficult to accept Lohmeyer's view, shared by Raymond Brown, that the primary focus of the prayer has to do with relationships within the church. Not only does that view conflict with a major thrust of Jesus' teaching and the image of the messianic banquet where all sorts and conditions of persons sit down together, it restricts to a very limited group what has in fact been claimed as a prayer of faith for those for whom the church is a very limited reality. A prayer which belongs only to an inner core of disciples seems inconsistent with the larger message of the gospel as reaching out to those "in the highways and byways" who are uncertain where they belong and as such may indeed pray the prayer as an eschatological rather than a present reality.

As has been evident in the discussion thus far, there is a problem with human forgiveness not only for pastoral theologians who must wrestle with it with particular parishioners and clients, but also with New Testament scholars in their attempts to interpret the Lord's Prayer in the light of Jesus' teaching or Christian theology as a whole. Scholars have dealt with the problem in a variety of ways, only a few of which have been noted here. One of those ways is to accept our forgiveness of others as a condition of the Christian life or, as Bonhoeffer's early work suggests, one of "the costs of discipleship." Another way is to resolve the problem through emphasizing the eschatological interpretation of the prayer to the extent that most expectations of forgiveness are shifted to the future. The tension between now and then is substituted for the tension of the relationship between our forgiveness and God's. Another resolution is one in which the human condition itself precludes any significant expression of forgiveness except as a reflection of the forgiveness of God. All of these resolutions seem to me to merit our attention, but none of them alone deals adequately with the problem of human forgiveness as I have experienced it in pastoral counseling.

My own view, which is based as much upon pastoral theological concerns as New Testament interpretation, is that the meaning of the petition about forgiveness in the Lord's Prayer is often obscured because it is interpreted apart from the total message of the prayer. Viewing the prayer as a whole requires that all the petitions be understood in the light of our relationship to God as *Abba* now and in the future.

David Norris's study of human forgiveness in the New Testament grows out of a concern similar to mine—bringing insights from clinical practice into dialogue with theological meaning. Norris makes use of Rudolf Bultmann's article on *forgiveness* in Kittel's *Theological Dictionary of the New Testament* to present the basic sense of the word as "sending off, releasing and letting go, especially in its legal

ἀπολύω

aspects." The Aramaic which Jesus himself would have used is parallel in its basic meanings: "to let go, to leave, to leave behind." Thus, in the light of this meaning of the word in the New Testament, forgiveness would seem to come about through a process of "releasing, surrendering, or letting go."[23]

In the Lord's Prayer, then, "to have debts forgiven is to be released from the burden of them." Moreover, because our obedience to God is profoundly connected to our relationships with one another, the forgiveness petition can be understood "both as a summons and as an invitation. It is a summons to the difficult task of releasing our claim to the right of judgement against each other. . . . And," Norris continues, "it is simultaneously an invitation to share in the greatest of God's gifts: the act of forgiving, of releasing others from their burden of guilt toward us." On the other hand, "To the degree to which we are unable to release others from their indebtedness to us we are also unable to know the depths of our forgiveness by God."

Norris does not, however, escape making human forgiveness a condition for receiving the forgiveness of God, for he says that if we are to know

> this release which God has promised . . . then we must release others from their burdens of indebtedness to us not because we ought to but because forgiveness cannot work for us otherwise. The constraints are not upon God, but upon ourselves, and the laws or principles involved are psychological and spiritual rather than moralistic.

More helpful, at least in my judgment, is his interpretation of the forgiveness petition as dealing not with what one ought to do but with "what is." It is "a description that recognizes the limitations of the human heart and that pushes us to acknowledge our final and complete dependence on the grace of God."[24] Thus he manages to come out where Lohmeyer does, emphasizing our dependence upon God, but without undercutting the responsibility for our brothers and sisters which is inescapable in Jesus' teaching. Perhaps because he comes to the issue of human forgiveness out of the practice of pastoral counseling where more time must be spent with the "is" than with the "ought," I find Norris's work to be particularly helpful. And in dealing more effectively with the "is" he is able to maintain the tension between the "now" and the "to come" that is emphasized by most of the recent interpreters of Jesus' teaching.

Other Pastoral Counselors and Human Forgiveness

As a pastoral counselor, I am not alone in my concern to examine some of the problems with human forgiveness. David Norris, whose work I have been discussing, and David Augsburger are fellow pastoral counselors who make use of that competence in their writings. I have many areas of agreement with both of them, although the major contention of this book differs from their points of view. Although Norris makes a number of contributions to the understanding of human forgiveness, the primary one, in my judgment, is his description of human forgiveness as a process. He uses biblical materials in his argument, but his work as a pastoral counselor and his understanding of both psychodynamic and family therapeutic theory are the interpretive key for what he says. Although his discussion of the forgiving process is worthy of much more attention than I can give it here, the following is a brief summary.

First of all, according to Norris, human forgiveness requires the "intention to forgive." "What is important is that forgiving be consciously intended in the context of a presently felt injury . . . and it needs to relate to an injury that is being experienced to some degree in the present." The next step is "to recreate the experience of injury, with as much detail as possible," including "what happened to cause the wounding" and "how the injured person personally experienced the injury. . . . The step which requires the greatest amount of therapeutic work is typically that involving release of the negative energy that has collected around the experience of injury or been triggered by it and that prevents the inner forces of healing from transforming it."

A further step which happens along with the two just ③ described is "the reconstruction of meaning." Forgiveness "involves a letting go not only of the negative energy connected with an injury, but also of the meanings which were learned as a result of that and similar injuries throughout one's life." Next is the repairing of relationships from the past that have been found to be recapitulated in the present. It is not so much a forgiving of persons in the past along with those in the present as a reconceptualizing of one's past relationships in the light of new knowledge. The final step is "reintegration in a more loving way of those parts of the self that had been isolated by earlier experiences of injury."[25]

Norris summarizes his interpretation of Jesus' teaching on human forgiveness in the following way. First, human forgiveness is required

> both as preparation for receiving God's forgiveness and as response to the fact of having been forgiven. For the follower of Jesus to be forgiving of others is an obligation without limitation as to frequency, duration, or degree.
>
> Second, to forgive is to release, to let go . . . or to leave behind . . . the anger and resentment which is occasioned by another's wrongdoing against us. This in turn involves giving up our claim to the right of judgment against each other.
>
> Third, forgiveness needs to happen at the deepest levels of the personality, "from the heart." It is not a superficial phenomenon.
>
> Fourth, one's capacity to love others deeply and freely is in itself evidence not only of forgiveness given but also of forgiveness received.
>
> Fifth, it is beyond the power of human effort alone to accomplish. . . .
>
> Sixth, forgiving one another is made possible by the deep reception of God's forgiveness, and is therefore ultimately the work of God in us.
>
> Finally, there is a profoundly reciprocal relationship between our forgiving one another and God's forgiving us.[26]

Norris concludes his dissertation with point-by-point comparison of the biblical and psychotherapeutic steps he has identified, an identification of some biblical clues for expanding clinical awareness, and finally, by acknowledging some significant points of tension between biblical and psychotherapeutic points of view which must be left without resolution, such as Jesus' teaching on the conflict between family loyalties and the costs of discipleship. All of his work is interesting and stimulating. I comment only upon the portion of it which seems most relevant to my purposes.

In looking at any series of steps or stages, it is important to recognize that they are most useful as guides to illuminate our thinking rather than as categories to confine it. Both the biblical and psychotherapeutic steps in forgiveness which Norris identifies have elements that are sequential and others that seem to be simultaneous with one or more of the others. Repairing relationships from the past, for example, may occur prior to, simultaneous with, or after a person's intention to forgive is perceived. Although all of the steps are thought-provoking with respect to the problem of human forgiveness, it is important to recognize that they are not necessarily equal in importance or directly comparable because of the different ways in which they are derived. To say, for example, that forgiveness "needs to relate to an injury that is being experienced to some degree in the present" is an observation based in clinical experience, whereas to conclude that "one's capacity to love others deeply and freely is in itself evidence not only of forgiveness given but also of forgiveness received" is a judgment made on the basis of faith and theological understanding rather than observation. Both types of comment are useful, but it is important to recognize their differences.

My concern here has been to present some of Norris's conclusions because of the value that they have in stimulating our thought about the nature of human forgiveness as a process with a number of distinct but related elements, not simply as an act that is done or not done. Some of these elements seem more important to me than others, but those judgments will become evident as I summarize my own position. Before I continue, however, it seems important to identify one of Norris's steps which seems directly to conflict with my view of human forgiveness. It is his conviction that for forgiveness to take place "an intention to forgive is required." This judgment seems to me to be in danger of bringing back the moralism and works righteousness that Norris successfully avoided in his New Testament interpretation. An intention to forgive seems comparable to being an act one should try to perform. In focusing upon a particular action, it is easy to lose sight of the condition of the person who is to carry it out and look at the action alone. I believe, in contrast, that human forgiveness becomes possible by not trying to forgive and that this latter view is consistent with both the struggles of my counselees and a reasonable interpretation of forgiveness in the New Testament.

David Augsburger makes his contribution to the discussion of human forgiveness first of all through the visual presentation of his book as two books, each with its own cover, bound together in one: *Caring Enough to Forgive* on one side and *Caring Enough to Not Forgive* on the other. It is one of a series of books on caring that speaks persuasively of the danger of superficializing forgiveness: one cannot really care if forgiveness is understood to be easy or talked about too glibly. I myself find the *Caring Enough to Not Forgive* side of the book the more satisfying and the one to which I would refer specifically in suggesting the book to persons consciously dealing with this issue.

Augsburger identifies in useful, everyday language circumstances under which persons should care about themselves and those who have injured them. The first of these is when "forgiveness" (put in quotation marks to make his point that it is not true forgiveness) "puts you one-up." Here he is dealing with similar circumstances to those which I presented in the discussion of the defense of power. In fact, although he does not emphasize the concept of defense, what he presents as circumstances under which one should not forgive are for the most part descriptions of defenses used and denied. He takes seriously the way "forgiveness" can be a distortion and denial of reality by distorting feelings, particularly the feeling of anger, and makes a particularly useful contribution in his discussion of "forgiveness" used as a way of terminating or closing a relationship rather than opening it up. "I'll forgive him, but that finishes the transaction. I don't care enough about the other person (or myself) to keep bothering with this."

True forgiveness, for Augsburger, is never the end of something. It is a step along the way to reconciliation. As he puts it,

> Biblical agape is equal regard which refuses to stand one-up over another or to live in denial, avoidance or distance. Thus it continues loving and living out the works of love as an invitation to the genuine mutuality of forgiveness. It sees the real focus of forgiving not in individual release from guilt and proof of goodness, but in interpersonal reconciliation, wholeness and life together in Christian community.[27]

The real work of forgiving "is found in regaining the sister and brother as a full sister, as a true brother." Augsburger, in keeping with his Mennonite tradition, believes strongly in a healing community. Forgiveness is possible "not because of the benevolent superiority of the forgiver, but because of the choice to be transparent to the forgiving possibility that is present in the community that supports, sustains, stimulates one even in the midst of tragedy."[28]

Because forgiveness can be identified with a particular act and is often assumed to be an end in itself, Augsburger's affirmation of reconciliation as the end toward which forgiveness leads is an important reminder. I believe with him that reconciliation between God and humankind is the good news of which the gospel speaks, and our forgiveness by God and of each other is a witness to that reconciliation. Moreover, I can affirm the possibility of, and sometimes the actuality of, Christian community. I am much more skeptical, however, of the existence of an ongoing healing community in the church or for that matter in any one place. Human brokenness seems to me to be radical enough that to claim healing community to be in any one place is a distortion similar to the distortion of forgiveness of which Augsburger speaks. But that is another issue. It seems important now to return to where we started—to Emmie and Tom, and later to Herman and Hilda. What does all of this theological discussion have to do with these ordinary people with ordinary human hurts?

My Counselees' Concern with Forgiveness

If we were to ask them if they were concerned with being able to forgive, I suspect that Emmie and Tom and, perhaps, Herman and Hilda would say, "Not much." Emmie came to pastoral counseling to deal with her pain and her survival as a person. Her whole way of living and thinking about herself had been changed. She was aware that she needed someone to help her get through the time ahead, but the issue of her forgiving came up only through the sermons she heard in church, which she rejected, and in her relationships with her children. Their continuing to care for their father created tension and brought into her thinking the issue of forgiving them for what appeared to her to be their disloyalty.

The thought of forgiving Elmer, however, seemed to come nowhere near her consciousness. For many months she clung tightly to her innocence in the whole matter, maintaining what I have called the defense of righteousness. The process of pastoral counseling involved developing a dependable, caring relationship that attempted to be more responsive to her pain than to her rage at Elmer. The pain that she was experiencing now in her life was gradually related to other pain which had occurred earlier—her struggle to get her mother's blessing, her affection for but unsuccessful competitiveness with her sister, her feelings of being contingent upon everyone else's wishes. She acknowledged that she had been dissatisfied with many things about the marriage but had done nothing to try to improve them. It gradually became clear that Elmer's leaving was not just "out of the blue" but had grown out of a longtime dissatisfaction. She had avoided bringing the issue to a head, but had just hoped that it would go away and continued to try to please Elmer as she had learned to try to please others.

Throughout this process her righteousness held strong and was the constant counterpoint to the gradually broadening issues of her life that she was willing to consider with me, i.e., we moved from the rage and shame of her rejection by Elmer to the older inadequacy and shame she felt in relation to her sister and her mother. Pastoral counseling became concerned with her self and her life and how she had dealt with it, not just with her present feelings and circumstances. As this process continued, the contrapuntal note of her righteousness remained but was reasserted less frequently. I felt concern about her continuing caughtness in rage and righteousness, but made the judgment that addressing them directly as evils to be excised was far less important than her rediscovery of who she was in the context of our relationship.

In reflecting upon my own theoretical formulation at the time, I am aware that I shared some of the common assumptions, discussed in an earlier chapter, that it would be a good thing if she could get rid of her rage, forgive Elmer, and get on with her life. I am further aware of the power of suggestion in a relationship as important as ours was to her, and I recall my thoughts that as a minister of the gospel I ought to be able to heal or at least comfort her with words I both represented and believed: "You are forgiven; you are released to be forgiving." My understanding of my role and function said to me, however, that although I might be able to preach that particular gospel from the pulpit in her church, to state it as a fact in the context of our counseling relationship was to remind her of her inadequacy rather than to strengthen her for discovery. Part of the bind of the pastoral counselor's role is that he or she is limited to asking, "Do you see the good news?" rather than announcing it as a fact. In a depth relationship with an individual or a family, a statement of even the best good news is often experienced as a confirmation of inadequacy because it is only the "all wise and knowing one" who has been able to see it that way.

What I did, as is evident from the interview fragment I presented, was to wait until there were signs that Emmie was seeing something different in Elmer and herself and then point, in terms close to her own experience, to the "larger gospel" of a common humanity: "Elmer seems almost human." Perhaps this seems inadequate as a verbal expression of the good news that we are forgiven and can thereby be forgiving. As I see it, although the words may not seem as impressive, they may be more important. In Emmie's case a relationship with me allowed her to rebuild enough of who she was that she could experience herself and present herself to others as a full person. As such, her need for the defense of righteousness lessened, and she could experience some of the same adulterous urges that people like Elmer have. I do not believe that it was important for her to say that she *forgave* Elmer. What was important, and what to me is the "larger gospel," is the discovery that Elmer is human like herself. This is forgiveness as discovery rather than as act.

In Tom's situation the concept of forgiveness, as part of his defense of power, is present throughout his counseling with me. Vulnerable to a powerful father who could do apparently arbitrary things like leaving his family, Tom draws upon his early experience in the church to develop his fantasies about forgiving. It is certainly not his only defense, but it is a particularly useful one with a father who, though strong, is anxious to please his son. The father wants to be forgiven. The problem as it appears with persons who are aware of and concerned with forgiveness is that both the giving and receiving of it maintain the role of being one up on the other. This is why I said to Tom, as he speculated on whether or not he could forgive his father, "You sound more like a priest than a son." My concern was to confront him with his defense of being one up on his father and question whether or not he still needed that in the way he once did.

I directed him to go back to the feeling of the lump in his

throat because that seemed to be an expression of his feelings of closeness to and identity with his father. He was discovering how much they were alike but resisting that discovery by holding on to his old and familiar distancing mechanism—whether he could forgive or not. Although I believed in the importance of forgiveness, I was experiencing that verbal speculation about forgiveness as resistance to realizing that he was already forgiving. Perhaps my sarcasm was my own defense against feeling too much excitement and warmth about what I perceived as going on. I think it was also a way of allowing Tom to come to an awareness of his forgiving in a gradual way, not getting hung up on this religious thing he might be doing—forgiving—but getting at it through experiencing his father's humanness and his own—again, "the larger gospel."

Another aspect of this view of forgiveness may be seen in the situation of Jack and Joyce. A couple in their early thirties who had been married about seven years, they were referred to me by their pastor because of Jack's career dissatisfaction and unresolved grief over his father's sudden death. As I became acquainted with Jack and Joyce, something of their marital role pattern began to emerge. They had established role functions with each other in which Jack was the serious and withdrawn person, the patient in the marriage, whereas Joyce was the happy healer and social director. One could say without too much distortion that, in addition to the problem they presented at first, they had come for help in order to get out of the rigid roles which they had unconsciously developed for themselves. To verge on caricature for emphasis, Jack was angry with Joyce for being too happy and not having things bother her. Joyce was angry with Jack for seeing the dark side of everything.

During the process of counseling, which involved getting in touch with a variety of old and new feelings and—particularly in Jack's case—expressing them much more than ever before, Jack began to raise questions about Joyce's premarital sexual experience. The fact that she had been sexually involved with another person prior to her marriage to Jack had never been a secret and had apparently never bothered him before, but now as he was becoming increasingly aware and expressive of his feelings about everything else in his life, his curiosity and anger about the details of Joyce's earlier life seemed to obsess him. Joyce continued in her role of trying to be helpful and attempted to allow Jack to get it out of his system. Instead of decreasing or disappearing, however, the anger and tension seemed to increase for both of them. Things got worse instead of better.

The theme of the latter portion of the case fragment is familiar because of its appearance in the newspapers in "Dear Abby" and her counterparts, most often in form of, "Should we confess all of our sins and premarital experiences before we get married?" Would things have been better if Joyce had decided to go over the details of her sexual history with Jack earlier in their relationship? To answer no is not as important as seeing the assumption behind the question—that confessing and being confessed to is always good and helpful. It is not. Another popular assumption revealed by the situation is that if one finds and reveals the offending material, things will get better. Freud in his early work seemed to have a similar assumption, searching like a neurologist for an offending lesion which could be treated or removed. Later, it became clear to him that this was only part of the "cure."

There is often a similar assumption about human forgiveness. Applied to the case of Jack and Joyce, it would be something like this: If Jack will only forgive Joyce for her permarital sexual experience with another person, he will be released from his need to hurt himself and her with that experience, and their relationship will develop into a more open and trusting one. In my experience it not only "ain't necessarily so," it is not likely so. But, as this common assumption goes, if Jack and Joyce were the kind of people they ought to be—really good Christians—then surely this would be the case. In the special relations within the family—where my experience lies—good Christians are not any better at this kind of forgiveness than anyone else.

[171]

My assumption in working with Jack was that his obsession with Joyce's prior sexual experience had to do with his deep fear of not being able to get from her the kind of intimacy that someone else had experienced. In their marital balance, Joyce had gotten locked into the role of social director, trying to make Jack happy and pull him out of his sadness and isolation. In doing so, she presented herself as someone successful with everyone and everything and really bothered by nothing. It often appeared that she had all she needed from life without Jack. She helped compensate for his seriousness but angered him by dealing with life in a way that appeared superficial. He needed a deeper intimacy with her in order to handle the pain of his father's death and his fear of not being able to live up to his own and others' expectations of him. His ineffective way of dealing with this need was to attack Joyce for possibly giving someone else something that he hadn't been able to get from her.

Jack's need is not so much to know Joyce sexually as to know her depth as a person. His need is not to forgive her for having experienced sexual things with another person, but after he has come to know her in a deeper way, to "forgive" her for the anxiety and lack of understanding which caused her to hold out on him. In this case the forgiving comes not from doing any one thing or forgiving a particular sin but from Jack's discovering his own humanity and finding that Joyce's humanity is really a lot like his own—not better or worse, above or below. The problem with human forgiveness in special relations is that when forgiveness is understood as doing something or not doing something, it is virtually impossible to avoid being above or below the other or to escape the roles of priest and penitent—roles which maintain separation rather than facilitate intimacy.

The defensive use of the priest and penitent roles may be seen in Patti, a woman who had had an abortion. She decided to do this, as she remembers it now, because her husband did not want another child and because she was constantly ill during pregnancy. The discussion of her feelings about the abortion occurred several months into our counseling relationship, which had begun with Patti's presenting a variety of other concerns. As she struggled with her feelings, Patti said, "I just don't think I can ever forgive myself for having that abortion." My response to her statement was something like this: "It sounds like you have decided to be both priest and penitent. I wonder what each of those roles is doing for you."

What I said did not seem to be of much use to her at the time. It was more of a speculation than a response to her immediate feelings. The image of the priest offering forgiveness, however, was a familiar symbol to Patti, who was an active Episcopalian, and as time went on it became an increasingly useful way to talk about one of the ways that she defended herself against the change she said she wanted. She was the priest, who in spite of what she had done, stood for doing what was right and was uncompromising in her expectations of the penitent. If she could not do the right thing, she could certainly identify herself with it and in doing so feel more power than powerlessness. But she was also the penitent, someone who had done such an awful thing that she could not be expected to change and live a better life than she was living now. As such a sinner, what she could do about her life was limited, as was the risk that she might have to take to make any changes. Both the moral priest and the immoral sinner helped her maintain the status quo—unforgiving and unforgiven—and without the responsibility of a sinner who has realized forgiveness and is going on with her life.

Forgiving by Not Trying To

My concern now is to pull together some of the elements of the chapter into an affirmation about human forgiveness and its relationship to God's forgiveness. That the New Testament has an important message about human forgiveness is clear. Just what that message is, however, is not. At least it is subject to significant distortion if it is not examined in relation to Jesus' central message about the kingdom of God and a realistic appraisal of the way human beings are, rather than the way we wish they were. My conclusion as a pastoral theologian from reviewing data both from interpreters of the New Testament and from the struggles of my counselees is that human forgiveness cannot be ignored but should not be focused upon as something one should do. "Forgive us our debts as we forgive our debtors" must be taken seriously, but not separately. The message about human forgiveness in the Lord's Prayer is found not by extracting from its context the one petition in the prayer that seems to tell us what to do, but in seeing that petition, like the others, as essentially an affirmation of God's relationship to us.

The Lord's Prayer in Luke's Gospel is placed in the context of the disciples' childlike request to Jesus to teach them how to pray. And when he does, that same childlike relationship is described in the prayer. As children of God they are told to express themselves by acknowledging their dependency in a personal way. They are to address God as *Abba*, convey their sincere expectation of the kingdom's coming, acknowledge that even their daily bread comes from him, trust in his forgiveness and the forgiving quality of human life that is possible because of it, and expect his presence with them in the inevitable trials of life. As a number of interpreters insist, the prayer is eschatological. It is an expression of faith about the way things are in the kingdom, in a fragmentary way now, and the way we trust they will be when it comes in its fullness.

Interpreting the prayer as an expression of personal relationship to God, of dependency and human finitude, reduces the possibility of its being used as an excuse for human power and claims of righteousness. Forgiving is not something that we have the power to do or are righteous in doing, but a description of the nature of our now-and-to-come kingdom relationship to God and to one another. Like God's kingdom, forgiveness is something that is discovered to be "in the midst of us," as a part of our neighbor-hood with one another. The New Testament image which most powerfully expresses it is the messianic banquet, where strange dinner companions sit side by side at a common table. Their differences are obvious, but seated at the same table they are able to see how they are like each other. When, as in the cases of Emmie and Tom, someone who has injured us and whom we have only been able to see in terms of that injury is found to be human in some of the same ways that we are human, we have discovered forgiveness, and something of the kingdom is present among us.

One of the qualities of special relationships is that their specialness contributes to the difficulty of seeing what is not special about the other person. The day before I wrote this, one of my counselees told me with surprise that he thought he was beginning to see his wife for the first time as an independent person—someone who had a life of her own and who was a person a lot like himself. Viewing this discovery from the outside, it is difficult to understand why it took so long or why it is so important. Viewing it in relation to the persons who are special to us, we may see some of the same slowness in ourselves. My own life experience and my experience with others in pastoral counseling tell me that we spend the great majority of our time responding to the roles and functions a person has in relation to us rather than to the way he or she is as a separate human being. Human forgiveness involves at least a momentary seeing beyond our relationship to a wife, a husband, a child to one who is a person in the same way that we are.

seeing beyond family roles

The point of view that I have been expressing, then, affirms the importance of human forgiveness, but insists that it is a quality of the kingdom to be discovered, not something to be done to improve our health or salvation. I certainly make no claim that this is the only way to understand the teaching about forgiveness in the New Testament. I do believe, however, that what I have said is not inconsistent with that teaching and is, moreover, a useful interpretation of the predicament and possibility of human beings as I encounter them in pastoral counseling. In the concluding statement about the problem with human forgiveness which follows this chapter, I relate this point of view to the various questions with which we have been left in the previous five chapters, suggesting some of the practical implications of understanding human forgiveness *not as doing something but as discovering something—that I am more like those who have hurt me than different from them. I am able to forgive when I discover that I am in no position to forgive. Although the experience of God's forgiveness may involve confession of and the sense of being forgiven for specific sins, at its heart it is the recognition of my reception into the community of sinners—those affirmed by God as his children.*

Notes

1. Norman Perrin, *The New Testament: An Introduction* (New York: Harcourt Brace Jovanovich, 1974), p. 288. A very useful summary of the authentic sayings of Jesus is found in David Abernathy's *Understanding the Teaching of Jesus* (New York: The Seabury Press, 1983), pp. 203-19. Abernathy, whose primary field of ministry has been in communication rather than New Testament scholarship, has, in my judgment, made a valuable contribution in this book by making results of critical scholarship, primarily from the point of view of the late biblical scholar Norman Perrin, available to the layperson in a way which appears supportive to faith and religious devotion. The particular section noted here is an appendix to the volume which presents those sayings most consistently viewed by scholars to be those of Jesus himself rather than additions and interpretations of the writers of the Gospels.

2. Perrin, *New Testament,* pp. 289-91.

3. Abernathy, *Understanding the Teaching of Jesus,* p. 50.

4. Norman Perrin, *Rediscovering the Teaching of Jesus* (New York: Harper & Row, 1976), p. 107.

5. Norman Perrin, *Jesus and the Language of the Kingdom* (Philadelphia: Fortress Press, 1976), p. 30.

6. Ibid., p. 47.

7. Ibid., pp. 198-99.

8. W. A. Quanbeck, "Forgiveness," *The Interpreter's Dictionary of the Bible* E–J:318.

9. Perrin, *Rediscovering,* p. 126.

10. C. F. D. Moule, "The Christian Understanding of Forgiveness," in *From Fear to Faith: Studies of Suffering and Wholeness* (London: S.P.C.K., 1971), pp. 61-72. Moule's central concern in his writings on forgiveness is to argue that "in a Christian understanding of the way in which offence and estrangement are dealt with, there is *no place at all* for retribution." Forgiveness, therefore, must be dealt personally and without calculation of obligation and justice.

11. David Amherst Norris, "Forgiving from the Heart: A Biblical and Psychotherapeutic Exploration" (Ph.D. diss., Union Seminary, 1983 [Ann Arbor: University Microfilms International]), p. 81.

12. Joachim Jeremias, *The Central Message of the New Testament* (New York: Charles Scribner's Sons, 1965), pp. 20-21.

13. Ibid., p. 28.

14. Norman Perrin, *The Kingdom of God in the Teaching of Jesus* (Philadelphia: The Westminster Press, 1963), p. 192.

15. Raymond Brown, *New Testament Essays* (Milwaukee: The Bruce Publishing Company, 1965), p. 253.

16. Perrin, *Kingdom,* p. 195.

17. Ibid., pp. 196, 201-2.

18. Brown, *New Testament Essays,* p. 248.

19. Ernst Lohmeyer, *"Our Father": An Introduction to the Lord's Prayer,* trans. John Bowden (New York: Harper & Row, 1965), pp. 170, 171, 173.

20. Ibid., pp. 181-82.

21. Friedrich Hauck, in Gerhard Kittel's *Theological Dictionary of the New Testament,* trans. Geoffrey W. Bromiley (Grand Rapids: Wm. B. Eerdmans, 1964-72), 5:562.

22. Norris, "Forgiving from the Heart," p. 72.

23. Ibid., pp. 56-57.

24. Ibid., pp. 76-77.

25. Ibid., pp. 150-54.

26. Ibid., pp. 184-85.

27. David Augsburger, *Caring Enough to Forgive/Caring Enough to Not Forgive* (Ventura, Calif.: Regal Books, 1981), pp. 6-7.

28. Ibid., pp. 80-92.

Reflections
and Implications

My concern now is to reflect briefly upon some of the issues that have emerged in the discussion of different aspects of the human forgiveness problem and to suggest some of the pastoral implications of what has been said. The common understanding of human forgiveness is that it is an act to be performed and/or an attitude to possess. One identifies himself or herself as Christian by doing the act or having the attitude. If one doesn't forgive or have the attitude of forgiveness, then he or she is simply not trying hard enough and should try harder. My discussion of the problem has pointed out some of the limitations of this view and suggested an alternative which I believe is more in keeping with life as it is and consistent with Jesus' teaching about the kingdom in the New Testament.

How Often Shall I Forgive My Brother?

The humanness in that question expresses much of the problem I have been discussing—not so much trying to paraphrase the New Testament as understanding the question as a pastor might when hearing it from a parishioner. The question seems to say, "Please give me a rule so I don't have to keep dealing with this. How can I know when enough is enough? I want to know what to do instead of having to come to terms with the whole history of our relationship." The pastoral response—however it may be communicated—is that there is no rule to make the relationship simple. Jesus' response to the question was to say in effect, "I am unwilling to give you a way out of a continuing relationship to your brother."

In a very different context, Ivan Nagy seemed to be saying the same thing when he spoke of invisible loyalties. You cannot be free of your brother and your father and all those in special relation to you. There is at least a three-generation history that must be taken into account, and that history is not just one of external events which have been shared together, but all the feelings and thoughts about those events and what they have meant to the family. The human problem is not how to forgive, if this is understood as something to be done, but finding a way to discover that the brother is a human being like oneself in spite of all that may have happened in that relationship. Forgiveness numbered and accomplished can be a way out of a relationship, whereas Jesus' answer to the question affirms the relationship and all it involves. Pastoral care and counseling, whatever its methodology, involves exploring the pain and possibility of the troublesome relationship.

Marriage also presents the challenge of living with, rather than limiting, the responsibilities of relationship but with the added complication that the marital partner represents one's own choice for achieving intimacy and creativity.* In the intimacy of reaching out to another there is a continuing possibility of disappointment and rejection, accentuated by fact that this failure to be fulfilled is a result of my marital choice, not the circumstances of my family of origin. Carl Whitaker's emphasis upon the irrational components in a marriage relationship is helpful in reminding us of the intensity of feeling which may be part of marital broken-ness. In marriage another dimension of my humanness is exposed to the possibility of shame.

---

*I believe that this is the case even with marriages which have in some way been arranged for the couple by others because in living the marriage there is a continuing opportunity to choose the other to fulfill oneself.

Human forgiveness here is related to, but not dependent upon, reconciliation taking place in the marriage. It involves discovering that there are ways for me to be whole in spite of my loss of part of myself in the loss of a marital partner. And when this "wholeness in spite of" becomes a possibility, there is also the possibility of accepting the humanness and wholeness of the other. Seeing the other as a person apart from his or her relationship to me is a major element in the meaning of forgiveness in a broken marital relationship. For the pastor, it suggests that his or her efforts in caring and counseling involve helping the counselee to focus upon his or her own self rather than upon what was lost in the other person. Rage and bitterness are overcome not so much by trying to do so, but by rediscovering myself apart from the other.

Another question that appears in reflecting upon the meaning of special relationships and human forgiveness is how the real and symbolic brother are related. Jesus' answer to the question, "And who is my neighbor?" has clear implications for the forgiving of the brother. The neighbor, the symbolic brother, is also the one whose relationship to you cannot be sought in a numerical answer. If human forgiveness in special relations involves discovering that in spite of how he has injured me, my brother and I belong to the same family and are, underneath all our differences, ultimately like each other, the same is true for the symbolic brother as well. Our task is not to calculate the limits of our liability, but to seek to discover our common history. Christian ministry involves assisting persons in this discovery.

Accepting Our Shame and Discovering Our Guilt

The extensive discussion of shame in chapter 2 has suggested but not developed the point of view that pastoral counseling involves helping persons accept their shame in order to discover their guilt. Although assisting persons to deal with unrealistic feelings of guilt is an important part of pastoral work, many of those struggling with human forgiveness are unable to see their real guilt—to be aware of their sin—because they are so fully aware of their shame. In the midst of the powerful and primitive experience of shame, persons are estranged from relationship, feeling that any human contact brings more exposure and, consequently, more shame. The primary pastoral task is bringing the shamed person back into relationship—with the pastor and with others. It involves what Kohut understood as using the therapeutic relationship to build self-structure or what Kaufman has called rebuilding the interpersonal bridge.

Shame, as we have discussed it, has been understood as an experience of the whole person. Sometimes the intensity of shame functions as a protection against the loss of boundaries by painfully defining who one is. In every case it is a response of the whole self to the experience of rejection and frustration. Guilt, in contrast, is a partial experience in the sense of involving one or more actions of the self rather than the whole self. The appropriate response for the pastor, then, is the offering of a caring relationship to the estranged and separated person, not a premature attempt to produce an act or attitude of forgiveness toward the one who has shamed him or her. When shamed persons overcome some of the isolation which their injuries produced, they can begin to see some of their own guilt and responsibility. As the experience of Christian worship suggests, one is able to accept oneself as sinner when one feels related and a part of community.

Another important thing to consider when attempting to offer care to a shamed person is that persons often speak of guilt when what they are experiencing is shame. The fact that both psychology and religion have emphasized guilt at the expense of shame contributes to the confusion. Much of the material in the chapter on shame was intended to help distinguish the two. Although in pastoral counseling, sharing the experience is much more important than using the right word, in this particular case using and interpreting the meaning of shame to one's parishioner or counselee can often help the person share and begin to overcome the shame that he or she is experiencing. It can be appropriate to pray, then, "Help us to accept our shame that we may discover our guilt," for our guilt represents responsibility for our actions to the community of which we are a part. As a member of that community and as we are aware of our relationship to significant others, we are able to acknowledge our responsibility for not doing the things that we ought to have done and doing the things that we ought not to have done. Although it is important to help persons get rid of the unrealistic feelings of guilt which may be an avoidance of a more important issue in life, the guilt which all of us have for our failures to live as we ought is actually a mark of our dignity and responsibility as human beings.

Pastoral Response to Rage

In the chapters on the defenses against shame, I gave extensive discussion to the rage a person experiences along with shame. I did this to emphasize the intensity of the shame experience and the threat to the self which narcissistic injury represents. The underlying rage involved is not something a pastor can address by trying to get the injured person to forgive or feel forgiving. The parishioner or counselee feels rage, not forgiveness, and it is simply not possible to substitute one for another. The caring response to such rage is neither to suppress it nor to try to force its expression, but to offer empathic understanding. Often this means a realistic but matter-of-fact interpretation of the consequences to the person or others if the rageful fantasies should be carried out. It involves a similar response to the one I have given my children in encouraging them to go ahead and express what they feel while they are at home, but reminding them of the danger of putting these rageful feelings into action against themselves, property, or other persons.

The pastoral response to rage is empathy for the impoverished self. That empathy is not so much warmth, although it may involve that, as it is a disciplined, intuitive understanding of the injured person that offers a model of a caring human being, useful information about oneself, and genuine experience in relationship. Although training and experience are important, a pastor does not have to be a trained psychoanalyst or be involved with a person in long-term psychotherapy in order to offer that understanding. What is most important is a genuinely human offering of oneself to the other person—not to what he or she has done or not done—with all the skill and expertise one has in human relationship.

Surrendering the Power to Forgive

I have suggested that a pastoral response to the problem with human forgiveness is not encouraging persons to forgive. It is enabling them to surrender their power to do it. My comment to Tom that he sounded more like a priest than a son points to the danger of viewing human forgiveness as something which one has to offer and which makes the one who has it somehow above the person to whom it is to be offered. This is why it is so easy to use forgiveness defensively. Though I feel rejected by, and thus below, the person who has injured me, in being able to forgive the injury I am really above him or her.

In affirming the importance of the community of faith and reconciliation with that community, the church in its mediation of forgiveness has often communicated that it was in a position of power—holding in its hand the means by which a person can overcome estrangement and be restored to fellowship. Those who have been influenced by the church have, therefore, sometimes learned to think of forgiveness as a power which they can possess. Thus the church has often contributed to the problem with human forgiveness rather than helped to understand it.

The pastoral response to forgiveness used as power is to understand it as an expression of human need to protect oneself against rejection and shame. Power is being used as substitute for relationship. Concentrating on one's power to forgive or whether one can or cannot forgive narrows the focus to the consideration of forgiving or not forgiving and

[183]

thus helps avoid the painful experience of shame. The pastor's first concern is to recognize that the issue of whether I can forgive or not is a substitute for the main purpose—to assist the injured person re-experience the power of being human rather than the power of being able to forgive. Being human is recognizing that I am neither above nor below the one I can forgive. I am like him or her. I don't have to claim power or specialness to be loved and to be of value in God's world. Pastoral care and counseling attempts to facilitate this discovery, not the maintaining of specialness through forgiving.

The Irrelevance of Righteousness

Pastoral counseling assists persons to surrender their righteousnes in the same way that it addresses the defense of power. Jesus' parable of the Pharisee and the publican offers in the Pharisee a prototype of a person substituting his believed difference from others as a claim for God's special blessing. Persons who because of a painful injury to the self are uncertain of themselves are likely to look for affirmation in fact that they are the injured and innocent party. This righteousness is irrelevant to the help they are seeking. Faced with this situation in pastoral counseling countless times, I have tried to find ways to help people "bracket" their righteousness. It is not ultimately irrelevant. Fairness, responsibility, and all those other valuable characteristics which persons point to when they need something to prove their self-worth are important, but not as a means of repairing the injured self.

My righteousness is important only after I don't need it anymore. When it is important to others and not to me, it is an essential aspect of my relationships. I believe this is consistent with that view of righteousness in both Old and New Testaments which sees it as an expression of the whole soul or person rather than as particular acts directed toward an external standard. Those who through empathic care have been brought back into community and can experience themselves as more similar to than different from the injuring person are persons for whom righteousness can be important. From that position—the position of the publican in Jesus' parable, the one who can see himself as a sinner—doing the right thing is something to be sought after. Pastoral counseling, as in the case of Herman and Hilda, may involve bracketing righteousness until some of the pain of rejection can be overcome.

The married couple who have rediscovered their common humanity are free to work on responsibility and fairness in their relationshp. They can learn to do what is right for the other without having to prove their own righteousness by it. As a part of that effort, they are dealing with the goodness/badness balance in their relationship. In many cases one member of the couple seems to get stuck with being the good or responsible person. He or she takes on responsibility for all the stability while the partner is understood, often unconsciously, to be the one who produces all the excitement, the risk, and the uncertainty. Couples who work through their defensive need to carry out a rigid role in their marriage can find satisfaction in swapping roles and functions with each other. This exchange is possible only when there is a secure enough sense of self in each to allow for such flexibility.

Pastoral Caring and the Discovery of Forgiveness

The point of view that human forgiveness is a discovery rather than something to be sought after presents an interesting problem for pastoral care and counseling. If one believes that forgiveness is an authentic and central element in Jesus' teaching about the Christian life, it would seem to follow that pastoral care should involve the guidance of persons in how they should forgive. The understanding of human forgiveness as something discovered rather than something done, however, suggests that direct guidance in forgiving is, in effect, turning that forgiveness theologically into a work, an achievement, and psychologically into a behavioral technique of reducing the pain of self-injury.

The implication of forgiveness understood as discovery

rather than act is that pastoral caring is helping persons not with forgiveness but with the pain of being themselves. It is attempting to break the isolation of shame and rejection so that they are freed from their need to view themselves as victims of life and can accept responsibility for their lives and the guilt that goes with it. The pastor can think of his or her task as helping persons to accept and experience their shame so that they can be responsible enough to be guilty. It is from the position of being an ordinary, responsible human being that this discovery becomes possible. As those who have studied the creative process have found, we are more likely to discover something when we are not trying to prove anything. Emmie and Tom, Herman and Hilda are normative for the rest of us only in their exemplifying that discovery is possible for all sorts and conditions of human beings. Christian pastoral care for persons who desperately need to discover the "forgivingness" in themselves is not in helping them look for it. Similar to the New Testament image of seeking the kingdom, it is more likely to be found when we are not looking for it. As a result of overcoming our estrangement from others through a caring relationship or relationships, as our bitterness recedes, it may be found in the midst of us. Like praying for the kingdom and looking for the signs of its presence, the pastor's responsibility in the discovery of human forgiveness is to be open to its possibility and able to announce its presence when it seems to appear.

Thus, the function of church and ministry is not to supervise acts of forgiveness, but to provide relationships in which genuine humanity, including the possibility that I am forgiving, can be discovered. Human forgiveness is something more likely to be discovered when the pastor is not trying to help someone do it. When I can recognize what is like me, i.e., neighbor-hood, in another, I have either forgiven that person or discovered that forgiveness as something done is not the main point anyway.

Index

INDEX

INDEX

male shame — performance

female " — appearance, approval of authority